T·I·N·A

BART MILLS

NEW ENGLISH LIBRARY

First published in the USA in 1985 by Warner Books Inc.

A New English Library Original Publication, 1985

Copyright © 1985 by Publications International Ltd.

First NEL Paperback Edition December 1985

NEL Books are published by
New English Library,
Mill Road, Dunton Green,
Sevenoaks, Kent.
Editorial office: 47 Bedford Square, London WC1B 3DP

Printed and bound in Great Britain by
Cox & Wyman Ltd, Reading

British Library C.I.P.

Mills, Bart
    Tina.
    1. Turner, Tina   2. Singers——United States
    ——Biography
    I. Title
    784.5′0092′4   ML420.T9/

ISBN 0–450–05899–9

ABOUT THE AUTHORS

BART MILLS has written extensively on music and other entertainment-related areas for publications around the world including *American Film, Emmy*, and *The Los Angeles Times*. He was pop music critic for England's *Daily Mail* newspaper from 1975 to 1979, as well as music writer for the English edition of *Cosmopolitan* from 1975 to 1980. He currently lives in Manhattan Beach, California, with his wife and teenage children.

IAIN BLAIR is a Los Angeles-based entertainment writer whose work has appeared in a number of newspapers and magazines, including *BAM, The Chicago Tribune*, and *Rock Video Superstars*.

BILL DAHL is a Chicago musician and music scholar with a special interest in blues and r&b music. His articles have appeared in *Goldmine* magazine, *Living Blues*, and the *Illinois Entertainer*.

Publications International, Ltd. gratefully acknowledges the following photographers and photo sources for their contributions to this book:

Attila Csupo; Sam Emerson; James Kriegsmann; Debbie Leavitt/Pix Int'l; Ross Marino; Linda Matlow/Pix Int'l; Movie Still Archives; Paul Natkin/Photo Reserve; Michael Ochs Archives; Personality Photos; Phototeque; Ebet Roberts; Lisa Seifert/Star File; Ann Summa; Susan Wilson.

Cover photos: Ron Grover/Shooting Star.

CONTENTS

I INTRODUCTION   6

II TINA: THE EARLY YEARS   10

III IKE   16

IV THE REVUE HITS THE ROAD   24

V IKE AND TINA: THE BEST OF TIMES   34

VI THE STRUGGLE FOR SOLO SUCCESS   48

VII	IN THE RECORDING STUDIO	66
VIII	PRIVATE DANCER: THE COMEBACK	80
IX	TINA ON SCREEN	94
X	THE WOMAN BEHIND THE MUSIC	108
	SELECTED DISCOGRAPHY	119
	FILMOGRAPHY	126

CHAPTER ONE

INTRODUCTION

To survive, Tina had to be tough.
And she was.

Looking remarkably youthful after enduring a 25-year career often
marked by suffering and pain, Tina's triumphant comeback is a tribute
to her indomitable spirit.

In those days the backwoods and the backs of busses were full of them—singing, shouting kids whose vocal message came out somewhere between a curse and a prayer. Slicked down and robed up to sing in the choir, they could carry a tune right up through the rafters and halfway to heaven. But they could throw a song right out the window when they had things on their minds that didn't belong in church. Their voices were big because they had to be heard by the Lord. Their songs were harsh because these kids knew already that things in this world had a habit of not working out the way the Lord had intended. ·

These kids learned their songs on Sunday and adapted them to real life during the rest of the week; and it is in their gospel music that rock 'n' roll had its roots.

Gospel music was nurtured in the rural South. It went to market in border cities like Memphis and St. Louis. It migrated to the big job centers like Memphis and St. Louis. It migrated to the big job centers of the North. It got further away from the church and acquired a new name—rhythm and blues. But no matter how popular it got, nor how far it strayed from the red-dirt junctions (like Nutbush, Tennessee) that gave it birth, it never lost the gospel sound. It never lost its hand-clapping exuberance, its testify-to-Jesus sincerity, its big, belting, listen-to-me voice.

Tina Turner belongs to that tradition, and the recognition that has finally come her way reflects both her indomitable personality and the durability of her music. Essentially, she's been singing the same song for years, a song to tell the world, 'Ain't life a bitch?"

Today Tina insists that her music is not rhythm and blues but rock 'n' roll, and the distinc-

8

tion is important: r&b implies black and r&r implies white. White means crossover, and crossover means big bucks. Whatever she calls it, though, Tina's music is modern in the sense that it was made for the age of video—literally, it has to be seen to be believed. Few other performers can more effectively "sell" a song with movement, and it has been Tina's shake-it-or-forsake-it stage style that has done more than anything else to keep her career going. The way Tina moves gives credibility to the emotions she sings about. From sexual abandon to deep-soul dejection, from sweaty highs to bone-dry lows, Tina's dancing tells the true story of her songs.

And the story of her life. When she asks, "What's love got to do with it?" you know she's done the sort of living that entitles her to ask the question.

The little girl whose powerful voice entertained the faithful at church picnics is a shadowy figure in the past of today's Tina. That little girl's parents didn't stay together forever, the way they were supposed to. When Tina got pregnant, the man she loved didn't stay around, like he was supposed to. The man who put her on the stage didn't turn out to be the loving husband of her dreams. The music business rejected her every chance it got.

To survive, Tina had to be tough. And she was. Against all the odds she rebuilt both her career and her life. During the long struggle she was sustained by the faithfulness of her fans abroad and by the force of her conversion to Buddhism. She made it, but it took a long time, a lot of pain, and a lot of work. No wonder she said, when her comeback was ratified at the Grammy Awards ceremony on February 27, 1985, "I've been waiting a long time for this."

CHAPTER TWO

◇ ◇ ◇ ◇ ◇ ◇

TINA:
THE EARLY
YEARS

◇ ◇ ◇ ◇ ◇ ◇

"I was always what you might describe as glamorous-minded. I can't remember a time, for example, when I didn't paint my toenails."
—London Evening Standard, *1979*

Ike and the newly christened Tina Turner (née Anna Mae Bullock) circa 1960, following the release of their first hit, "A Fool In Love."

Nutbush, Tennessee, is a tiny, cross-roads town—the kind that doesn't show up on maps. It consists of a store, a filling station, and a church; farmers come to town for supplies, for gas, or for Jesus. Nutbush, Tennessee, was Anna Mae Bullock's home during the early years of her childhood.

Tina's 1973 signature tune, "Nutbush City Limits," gives a clear picture of the town. "Church house, gin house, schoolhouse, outhouse. . . . On Highway Number 19, the people keep the city clean." And from another verse: "Go to the fields on weekdays, go to picnic on Labor Day, go to town on Saturday, go to church every Sunday."

As she told the *Los Angeles Times* in 1984, "It was all there. There was an outhouse for whites which was painted all pretty, and even as a child I could see that our outhouse wasn't painted. So I remember Nutbush, Tennessee."

Anna was born in a hospital in Brownsville, the seat of Haywood County. The town is 50 miles northwest of Memphis and 150 miles west of Nashville along Highway 19 (now known as Interstate 40). Her father, Floyd Bullock, was a supervisor of the sharecroppers who farmed the rich white-owned plantation land, located near the Hatchie River just before it flows into the Mississippi. Her mother, Zelma, half-Cherokee on her mother's side, already had one daughter, Eileen.

The Bullocks weren't rich, but Tina doesn't recall ever feeling poor. As a young girl growing up in Nutbush, Tennessee, Anna Mae had a relatively pleasant life. The home she grew up in was clean and well kept, she told *Rolling Stone*. The children had their own separate bedrooms. Compared with many people in the small rural community, the Bullock family lived quite comfortably.

As soon as she was old enough, Anna Mae dutifully took her turn in the fields like everybody else, picking cotton and strawberries. Her school was one room up from being a one-room schoolhouse. "I was brought up as a country girl," she says.

"In all the local communities, the white people own the land and the black people work the crops," Tina told *The Face.* "Every day you went to the fields, whether you were doing just the regular cultivating or picking cotton. My daddy was the caretaker on the plantation. People worked for him and he answered to the boss. But I actually worked in the fields."

Little Annie—sometimes called "Teeny" or "Tina" because she was the baby and because it didn't look as if she would ever attain any great height—had a big voice. Her earliest memories involve singing at one place or another, especially at picnics. In third and fourth grade Annie was among the first children to be asked to get up and sing and dance at these community gatherings. She would vocalize and cavort around the stage, backed up by the traveling musicians drawn to such affairs by the prospect of a free meal. Blues and jump rhythms were the order of the day, as were imitations of B.B. King.

Her musical tastes were formed early. As she said in *The Face,* "I liked them all, except I liked the low-down dirty ones the best. All those really bluesy, naughty ones. I could see the women poppin' their fingers and dancin' along."

She also used to show off in Nutbush's only store, trying to fill her piggy bank by singing for the shoppers. In school, her vocal teachers gave her all manner of songs to sing, from traditional to opera. And rain or shine, Annie sang every Sunday with the church choir, a tradition that helped discipline her natural vocal gifts. Although she was a farm girl who knew the Baptist hymnal back to front and described herself as "a church girl," she listened to the radio and knew there was another life to be led in the city. As she said in the *London Evening Standard* in 1979, "I was always what you might describe as glamorous-minded. I can't remember a time, for example, when I didn't paint my toenails."

Her home was not a happy one. The Bullocks had moved from Nutbush to neighboring Riplea when she was nine, and a couple of years later, Annie's parents split up. Her father left for Chicago and her mother made a new life for herself in St. Louis. The Bullock girls remained in Tennessee, and stayed with a variety of relatives and friends of the family before they finally ended up living with their grandmother.

Annie's endless shuttle from one home to another through her mid-teens instilled in her the streak of independent-mindedness that sustains her even today. It was this feistiness that led her to show business in the first place, and it gave her the strength to stay in the business after her split with Ike.

She and Eileen decided that the lights weren't bright enough in Tennessee, and as soon as they were old enough, they went upriver to live with their mother in St. Louis. "I always wanted to leave the fields," Tina said 20 years later while publicizing her *Rough* album. "Tennessee was fine—I loved sitting under a tree at the end of the day—but I knew there was more. That's why I joined my mother in St. Louis. To me, that was the big city."

At various times, Tina has ascribed different dates to her arrival in St. Louis. It may have been 1953; then again, it may have been 1955. Perhaps the problem stems from the confusion surrounding her birthdate, which she has variously said was 1938 or 1939. Tina herself is obviously bored by the age debate. "There's so much more to talk about. . . . It's as if that's all they want to know about me," she told *Reuters* in 1984.

In any case, she was in her mid-teens when she entered high school in St. Louis. She participated in a number of talent shows, and although she never won, she built up enough of a reputation that her school yearbook picture bore the caption, "Ann Bullock . . . entertainer."

Annie's interest in a career as a professional singer led her to the local music halls. She and Eileen used to stay out late at clubs where the show didn't start until after midnight. The pair's favorite haunt was a hot little spot called the Club Manhattan, over on the Illinois side of the river in East St. Louis, where the rules were a little looser than they were in Missouri. It was there that Annie, who was only allowed into the club because she looked older than she really was, saw a professional rhythm and blues band for the first time. The name of the group was The Kings Of Rhythm. The band's leader was Ike Turner.

CHAPTER THREE

◆◆◇◇◆◆

IKE

"Ike was a genius. Don't let anybody tell you anything different."
—Saxophonist Eddie Shaw

A slim man with a wispy goatee and slicked-down hair, Ike Turner was a multi-talented musician, producer, promoter, and talent scout. The only thing he couldn't do was sing.

Like so many of his blues contemporaries, Isaac Lustre Turner was a product of the musically fertile Mississippi delta region. Born in Clarksdale, Mississippi, on November 5, 1931, Turner was fascinated as a youth by the pounding boogie piano of Joe Willie "Pine-top" Perkins, Sonny Boy Williamson's accompanist on the legendary King Biscuit Time program over KFFA radio in Helena, Arkansas.

Young Ike convinced the pianist to teach him the fundamentals of the piano, but Turner's musical inclinations were more in the direction of jump bands like those of Louis Jordan and Amos Milburn. While still in high school, he assembled an 18-piece band called The Tophatters, which soon reformed with a pared-down lineup as The Kings Of Rhythm.

At the age of 16, Turner inaugurated a broadcasting career of his own at WROX in Clarksdale, spinning the latest r&b platters and taking note of any hot musical trends. He was also gigging on the side, tickling the keys behind the likes of Sonny Boy Williamson and slide guitarist Robert Nighthawk.

Sun Records was but a dream to Sam Phillips in early 1951. His Memphis Recording Service would produce sides by local blues artists and send them to major r&b labels, usually Chess in Chicago and Modern in Los Angeles. B.B. King, who cut his first Modern releases at Phillips' studio, caught Turner's act and told Phillips about the band. On King's recommendation, The Kings Of Rhythm set out for Memphis on March 2, 1951, to cut their debut sides.

Ike sang the first two himself, "Heartbroken And Worried" and "I'm Lonesome Baby." Then it was saxophonist Jackie Brenston's turn to sing. The band's other hornman, Raymond Hill, described the session in a 1979 *Blues Unlimited* interview: "They said, 'What you got, have you got any number of your own?' We said, 'Yeah, we got a song called "Rocket 88."' So we all got together, started putting some and thinking up some, piecing it together, see, it was—well, the recording of it was supposed to be the worst . . . the worst one come out the best." Hill supplied a storming tenor break on the catchy ode to the popular Oldsmobile, Kizart's guitar sounded fuzzy and distorted, almost like an electric bass, and the end result was what many historians now consider the first rock 'n' roll record. "Rocket 88" was an instant r&b chart-topper upon its Chess release, but Turner and Brenston soon had a falling out, and it was 1956 before they joined forces once again.

Turner began to pick up some recording session work around Memphis, and it was during one of his friend King's Modern dates that label head Joe Bihari hired the self-assured young pianist as his Delta talent scout.

Beating the bushes for unrecorded talent, Turner produced numerous blues artists for Modern and its subsidiaries, including Boyd Gilmor, Charley Booker, and Elmon "Drifting Slim" Mickle.

Chess had recently signed Chester Burnett, the Howlin' Wolf, and promptly scored a hit the first time out with "How Many More Years." But that didn't stop the enterprising Ike, who went right ahead and signed the Wolf for Modern anyway. Soon his records were appearing on two different labels simultaneously. Chess won the resulting litigation.

Turner produced some of the slide-guitar wizard Elmore James' earliest tracks, including one session in a Canton,

Mississippi nightclub. He worked with a young Bobby "Blue" Bland, whose star wouldn't rise for a few years yet. He even found time to put a few sides of his own, including a duet with his first wife, pianist Bonnie Turner.

By early 1954, Turner was working primarily out of Clarksdale, where he had established recording facilities. Ike's young nephew, Jessie Knight, Jr., had been added on electric bass to The Kings Of Rhythm, perhaps in an attempt to recapture the drive of Kizart's distorted guitar on "Rocket 88." Very few blues bands employed an electric bassist back then, and it gave the Kings a modern, driving sound.

Turner's prolific output in early '54 included sides with cohorts Billy Gayles, Clayton Love, and saxophonist Eugene "Sly" Fox, whose "Sinner's Dream" on Checker and "The Dream" on RPM were among the strangest records of their era, thanks to Turner's imaginative editing. Ike had been studying guitar with Kizart for about a year, and he was rapidly developing a brash, mean sound all his own.

Chicago tenor saxophonist Eddie Shaw was around for a few of the informal Clarksdale sessions as a youngster in nearby Greenville. "Ike Turner was a disc jockey at WROX in Clarksdale, and after the radio would go off the air, we would use the equipment to record on," recalls Shaw. "When Ike went off the air around 10 o'clock that night, we recorded all night until he had to go back on at six in the morning.

"Ike was a genius," adds Shaw, "don't let anybody tell you anything different."

Sometime in the summer or fall of '54, Ike left Clarksdale for good, allegedly after the local police shut down his studio for the "heinous" crime of fraternization with whites. The Kings Of Rhythm hit the road for East St. Louis, Illinois, and took nearby St. Louis by storm, rapidly developing into one of the city's hottest attractions.

Ike picked up right where he left off, producing artists for Modern including Johnny Wright, pianist Johnny "Big Moose" Walker, and a doo-wop group led by Art Lassiter called The Trojans. But by March of 1956, Turner and The Kings were signed to Cincinnati-based Federal Records, a subsidiary of the King label. The resultant 18 sides stand as the outfit's pinnacle—a series of remarkably powerful rhythm and blues songs.

Vocalist Billy Gayles' rich baritone shines on the rocking "Sad As A Man Can Be" and "Just One More Time." Knight's driving bass powers the shuffling "I'm Tore Up," which became a solid r&b hit, while "Let's Call It A Day" and "No Coming Back" showcased the singer's strong gospel feel.

Jackie Brenston was back in the fold, and he stepped up front for four tracks, including the raucous "Gonna Wait For My Chance." Clayton Love's four vocals ranged from the stomping "You've Changed My Love," with a fine tenor solo from Raymond Hill, to the minor-key novelty "She Made My Blood Run Cold." The remaining pair of tracks were instrumentals. On every song cut at the four sessions, the horns roar, the rhythm drives relentlessly, and Turner's guitar work is utterly fresh, wild, and frantic.

But one solid hit wasn't enough for Federal, and as the decade wound down, Ike was relegated to hawking his productions to a series of tiny St. Louis labels like Tune Town and Joyce. Tommy Hodge took over as principal vocalist, but there was a new girl on the scene, too. Making her debut on a somewhat bizarre group vocal effort called "Boxtop" was one Little Ann, who was still a couple of years away from being rechristened Tina.

Ike traveled back to Memphis in 1958 to sell his old friend Sam Phillips six sides, but Sun was in full blazing glory with its all-star rockabilly roster of such names as Jerry Lee Lewis, Johnny Cash, and Charlie Rich, and Phillips never got around to putting any of Ike's material out.

So the crew went north to Chicago and did two sessions for Cobra Records. Eight sides were captured, and the mixed lot ranged from straight blues stuff by Hodge ("I Know You Don't Love Me No More" and "Matchbox," both cut previously for Sun) to another version of "Boxtop," this time minus Little Ann, to the doo-woppish "Walking Down The Aisle." Turner left his rhythm section at home, using instead the everpresent Cobra A&R man Willie Dixon on bass and veteran Chicago drummer Odie Payne, Jr.

While they were in Chicago, Turner and his band backed a few of Cobra's artists, including young Betty Everett, and played behind two of the label's young West Side guitar giants, Buddy Guy and Otis Rush, appearing on a couple of Rush's classics, "Double Trouble" and "All Your Love (I Miss Loving)." But Cobra was on the verge of folding its tent, and only two Turner singles saw the light of day.

The entire Cobra outfit was recently reissued on the English Flyright label, and the package provides a fascinating insight into Turner's exacting recording methods. He proves to be a perfectionist throughout, going for take after take. On "You Don't Love Me No

More," he plays the piano intro himself, then reverts to guitar for the rest of the tune. Also intriguing is Turner's offhand remark at the end of the album: "We'll take this record round here to Chess, boy, and get us about $2,000, boy, and go to Florida!"

The band then returned to St. Louis and became involved in a short-lived liaison with Steven Records of Granite City, Illinois. His two releases on Stevens were issued under the pseudonym "Eki Renrut," apparently due to an outstanding contract Ike had signed with Sun.

In a remarkable 1981 *Blues Unlimited* interview, Thomas offers a candid insight into his ex-boss Turner's strict handling of his band. "He could put the boot in real good, he could really fire people, fine them and act crazy with them and stuff, oh yeah man, I've seen him do people wrong, but he would always have his justification and we believed he was right, me and Tina, that's why we was there all the time."

Sometime in late '59 or early '60, Ike scheduled a session for ex-Trojans lead vocalist Art Lassiter to cut a number called "A Fool In Love." But Lassiter failed to show, so Ike decided to try his new protégée, Little Ann, on the song. Ike sold the tape to Sue Records' Juggy Murray in New York, and the next phase of the multi-talented Ike Turner's career was underway.

Eddie Shaw sums it up well: "If there wasn't an Ike, there wouldn't have been any Tina."

CHAPTER FOUR

THE REVUE HITS THE ROAD

"After one year with Ike, I knew what he was really like. One thing stuck in my mind, 'When I've made him rich, I'll leave him.'"

Ike and Tina Turner in the early years: The band was constantly touring, but the hits were slow in coming. With the success of "River Deep, Mountain High" in Britain, however, the Turners found a audience eager for their music.

Accompanied by her sister Eileen, Anna Mae Bullock frequented the nighttime hotspots of St. Louis, and Ike's regular venue, the Club Manhattan was one of the Bullock sisters' favorite haunts. Annie was a big Ike Turner fan. "I just wanted to sing and dance so bad," she said in *Record* magazine, "and I loved Ike's band. His music was what my physical energy was. Whenever I heard that music, I was dancing."

Hungry for a chance to sing, Tina tried to take advantage of the fact that Eileen was dating Ike's drummer to wangle a chance to perform with the band. But Ike was understandably reluctant to let the 17-year-old high-school student front his band of seasoned professionals, so the answer always was no, not now, until. . . .

"One night, Ike was playing organ," Tina told *Club* magazine, "and the drummer sat a microphone on the table in front of my sister for her to sing. She said no, and I took the microphone and started singing. Ike told me later that he was shocked, but he finished playing the tune and then called me on stage."

The response of the audience was so overwhelmingly positive that Ike let her belt out a few more numbers before shooing her off stage. Soon, he was giving her a regular spot out front on the weekends.

For Tina, joining Turner's band was like being adopted by a new family. For a young girl accustomed to little family closeness, the Turner style of togetherness was a revelation. All six members of the band (and a steady supply of lady friends) shared a brick house in East St. Louis. Ike's common-law wife and their two children lived in the house as well, so Ike tended to carry on his extracurricular affairs elsewhere.

The Kings Of Rhythm was a traveling band that adapted its repertoire to suit whatever audience it happened to be playing for—the hit parade for jitterbugging white audiences, sophisticated harmonizing for the older, more mature black crowd, and down-and-jumping r&b for their true fans. For a night of performing in all these styles, Tina could pick up as much $15.

For the first time in her life, Tina felt like a star, she explained, recalling her introduction to stardom, mid-50s style, in *Rolling Stone*. Ike showered her with all kinds of fancy clothes and glittery jewelry for her stage show. The former country girl was overjoyed with her finery, and loved to get all decked out and drive around in Ike's pink Cadillac.

Tina's affections at this point in her career were reserved for Raymond Hill, who played the saxophone for The Kings Of Rhythm. Hill was Tina's first serious boyfriend, and her only one before Ike. "I started going steady with him in high school, and after him there was no one until Ike." In 1959, she bore Hill a son, Raymond Craig.

Ike didn't initiate a romance with Tina until he had a good reason to do so. He had broken up with the mother of his sons and decided to move the act to California. So he put his arm around Tina's shoulder one night and suggested a trip west.

Despite the fast company she kept and the lifestyle she led, Tina was no wild woman then. But she was susceptible where Ike was concerned. He was making her dreams come true, and it was not time to start saying no to him. "When Ike and I got together, I was very young. I was very much in love at the beginning. I went along, hoping Ike would change. He didn't, so I changed."

"My second year with Ike I realized I'd never be happy with him, and I wouldn't stay with him my whole life. After one year with him, I knew what he was really like. One thing stuck in my mind, 'When I've made him rich, I'll leave him.'"

Although she'd done some demo work earlier, "A Fool In Love" was Annie's first recording to see the light of day. Ike had written the song for a man's voice, but Art Lassiter, the vocalist designated to record the single, didn't make it to the session. Ike had paid for the time to cut a demo of the tune, and Annie was there, so she stepped in.

Ike had written other good songs during the 50s, but most of them had gone nowhere. "A Fool In Love" was his lucky break. The song, released on Sue Records in 1960, went to No. 2 on the r&b charts. Even more amazing was its showing on the pop charts, where it peaked at No. 27.

Annie soon discovered that working for Ike was not an easy way to earn a living. She contracted jaundice after recording "A Fool In Love" and spent six weeks in the hospital. "I was totally yellow," she told *Rolling Stone*. But Ike, wanting to capitalize on their first hit, talked Tina into sneaking out of the hospital and embarking on a tour.

On the basis of the hit and their ensuing record contract with Sue Records, Ike decided to turn his St. Louis-based Kings Of Rhythm into a Los Angeles-based national touring revue. He had attached the performance credit "Ike and Tina Turner" to "A Fool In Love" without telling Annie Bullock, who had no choice but to learn to like her new name fast.

The new name was more than just a whim on Ike's part. He was inspired by a popular comic book heroine, Sheena, Queen of the Jungle. She was a tawny lady who could swing on vines, fight wild animals, and out-yell Tarzan. Sheena was strong—no one got the better of her.

Thus, little Annie became the man-eating Amazon Tina. Her act was choreographed down to the last flutter of an eyelash to reflect Ike's vision of the jungle kitten. Even Tina's costumes emphasized the stripe motif. For many long years she pawed the boards in a little tigress suit that had more tail than top.

In a *New Musical Express* interview, Tina described the idea behind the act that she and Ike took on the road in 1960. "He'd always used two male singers. I thought we could get it on better with three females. I'd always danced, so that'd make it four. Then the *Shindig* show and white go-go dancing came along and gave us some more fuel. I wanted to break out of the limited plasticity of so many soul acts."

Tina's dancing was always carefully planned to look completely uninhibited. "The way I dance is the way I feel," she told the *London Evening Standard*. "I choreographed all my own dances, and they are all simple. The audience aren't dancers. They want to feel that they can do what I'm doing." Like her singing, her movements came out of the gospel tradition. She had attended a sanctified church in Knoxville, where worship was customarily accompanied not only by shouts, growls, and moans, but also by swaying, head-lolling, and sometimes even the all-out, full-body ecstasy.

If Tina was the preacher, then the Ikettes were her choir. The three backup singers and dancers, named in conscious imitation of Ray Charles' Raelettes, were the other half of Tina's call-and-response delivery. There were scores of Ikettes over the years. Among them were P.P. Arnold, Vanetta Fields, and Merry Clayton, who later had careers on their own. All the Ikettes were black, except for one brief stint served by white blues singer Bonnie Bramlett. Tina once said in *New Musical Express* that the Ikettes were always black because white girls couldn't handle the physically grueling work involved: "I find white girls are too frail and fragile to take what I put 'em through. They're always coming down with sniffles or bronchitis or fractures or something."

Ikettes couldn't be taller than the 5'4" star, nor could they be a lighter color. And they couldn't be prettier. "I don't want 'em too pretty-pretty," Tina said in *NME*. "Then they want to go out and be solo artists." An Ikette's salary would be docked if she ever stood between Tina and the audience or if she ever let a breast peek-a-boo out of its proper place.

The dancing by Tina and the Ikettes was sexy but not lewd. "Our dancing is half-stage and half-street," Tina told *NME*. "In spite of what everyone says, we try to keep it as clean as possible. No stripper bumps and grinds allowed. Notice, I always shoot the hips to the side, not to the front. No cheap shots."

Ike had always toned his music down for white audiences, so when Tina and the Revue played on mainstream stages, some of the steam was held in reserve. "I never felt we've used sex as a gimmick in our program," Tina told *Melody Maker* during the Ike days. "It's important today because people who pay to see a show want a little of everything. The sexual portion of our show isn't planned; it just happens.

"For years, we've gotten reviews that seem to dwell on the sexual aspect of the show. I've never felt people gaining sexuality from our show. But I like them to remember what they have just seen. I've never really thought of our show as being aggressive. Even as wild as I am, I know that I maintain my femininity. People have always told me that."

In a BBC interview during the Ike days, Tina said: "One of the first things your branded with, being black, is the bumping and grinding. We don't bump and grind. We bump, but we bump to the side. We do a clean show. They used to call it 'wild.' Now they call it 'energy,' and it's acceptable."

One of the highlights of the show in those days was her extended duet with Ike on "I've Been Loving You Too Long." Like many song titles, this one was suggestive enough in itself. The Ike and Tina stage rendition left no doubt as to what was being suggested.

In many ways, the show was structured like a revival meeting: Warm the congregation up to a fever pitch before letting the prime evangelist loose on them. The nine-piece band, billed at times as The Family Vibes, would start out with some instrumentals, often easing up to let Ike show off his distinctive snatch-and-grab-it guitar licks. Band members would pass the mike around for occasional solos. The Ikettes would come on and take turns soloing. And then, after a suitably prolonged wait and an introduction full of superlatives, the lights and volume would reach their full intensity and Tina would shimmy onstage, always in high heels, always at 100 percent intensity.

And she did it twice a night virtually year round from 1960 on. She was strutting her stuff even when she was six months pregnant with her second son, Ronnie, in 1962.

The pregnancy didn't please Ike. He went back to the mother of his other two children for awhile. However, he soon returned to Tina with the idea that they should get married immediately, Tina recalled in *Rolling Stone*. Although she didn't want to marry him, she was afraid to turn him down. So she and Ike went down to Tijuana, Mexico, and returned as man and wife.

A few black acts, like Chuck Berry and Little Richard, had scored big in the dawn of rock 'n' roll a few years before the Turners had come along. However, in the quiet years of the early 60s, it wasn't likely that a raucous r&b act like the Turners would build a large white following. The Ike And Tina Turner Revue did play Dick Clark's *American Bandstand* once in 1960, but most of their early performances were before black audiences.

"I was dressing like this star—fancy dresses, the high heels, and the furs and the gloves with the costume jewelry and the Cadillacs. I'd walk in with my head high, pretending. It was fun.

"That's as crazy as I got over it, because reality set in real quick," Tina told *Interview* magazine. "The clubs were uncomfortable. They were all very hot, with crowds of people and no ventilation. The perspiration would pour off us. I can remember standing and singing with circles of water at our feet, we were so hot. Just heat and smoke and of course in those days we did two shows.

"Every entertainer and movie star has felt like [quitting] at some time in their life. Certainly I did. Often. But what made me go on in those days was Ike. There was always

Ike. Music is Ike's life and what he wants. I am a part of Ike—that's what made me go on."

Ike and Tina had built a good career for themselves by the middle of the 60s. They had a solid track record on wax and a good reputation on the road. However, they missed the real surge of black rock 'n' roll performers into the mainstream via Stax in Memphis [Otis Redding] and Motown in Detroit. Ike had built his own bandwagon, but it was tiny compared with the crossover empires that had been built elsewhere.

Tina's records no longer interested the mainstream audience. The homogenization of black sounds for white ears by other artists kept her earthier efforts off the mainstream airwaves. But there was one successful producer who thought he could find a way to use Tina's rough and tumble style to score on the pop charts. He was Phil Spector. The song they recorded together, "River Deep, Mountain High," was exactly what everyone had hoped it would be—everyone, that is, but the American public.

CHAPTER FIVE

◆◆◆

IKE AND TINA: THE BEST OF TIMES

◆◆◆

"When I first heard Creedence Clearwater singing this song ["Proud Mary"], it just took me over. 'Ohhhh, that's the kind of song I want.'"
—Friday Night Videos, *1984*

Ike and Tina during the early 70s: The money was rolling in, but the magic was gone.

After the first flush of the British Invasion in 1964-65, when the American charts were overrun with songs by groups of long-haired Britons, a few people began to notice where the roots of this exciting "new" music lay. The Beatles, The Who, The Rolling Stones, and their imitators were clearly drawing inspiration from black r&b—a style of music that had never been widely popular in the States. The tunes and techniques that Ike Turner had helped create and perfect a decade and a half before were now playing their parts in the British-inspired renaissance of rock.

Although black r&b was at the core of the British Invasion, the black musicians who had pioneered the art form did not profit from its resurgence. Rhythm and blues could only find mass acceptance, as defined by steady airplay on the Top 40 radio stations and healthy record sales, if it was performed by whites trying to sound black or by blacks trying to sound white.

Ike Turner wasn't a compromising man. He was strongly committed to his music, and wasn't interested in changing his style simply to gain a wider audience. It took Phil Spector, a producer who had never before worked with a raw rhythm and blues singer like Tina Turner, to make the Turners' first significant connection to the mainstream, "River Deep, Mountain High."

By 1966, Spector was no longer the boy wonder who had turned The Crystals and The Ronettes into hitmakers while he was still a teenager. Spector's last successful group had been The Righteous Brothers, whose career nosedived in 1965. In May, 1966, he decided to revive his career by recording Tina Turner.

According to Tina in an interview with *Melody Maker,* "We were working around L.A. in 1966 and ran into Phil

Spector. He wanted to record me and when we cut "River Deep, Mountain High," Mick Jagger, who was visiting Phil at the time, was in the studio."

Conspicuously absent from the studio was Ike Turner. According to some accounts, Spector locked him out. In any case, Ike's contributions weren't welcome because it wasn't his song, and it wasn't going to have his sound. The sessions lasted two weeks (during which Spector was always very formal, Tina recalled in the *London Evening Standard*). Another single, "I'll Never Need More Than This," and an album, *River Deep, Mountain High,* were released later. Both were as unsuccessful as the "River Deep" single had been.

"River Deep," written by Spector, Jeff Barry, and Ellie Greenwich, was recorded in Spector's Wall of Sound style. Spector's sound, created through the use of heavy orchestration, a liberal amount of overdubbing, and lots of echo, was lush and dense. Tina's vocals were her best to date, fiery yet finely controlled, and more than a match for the grandiose production.

Perhaps radio programmers had it in for the reclusive, demanding Spector and conspired to bring about his downfall. Perhaps the record-buying public was tired of being beaten about the head and shoulders by the infamous Wall of Sound. Whatever the reason, Tina's big breakthrough didn't happen in 1966. The record was released and promptly fell flat. It reached no higher than No. 88 on the U.S. pop charts and didn't even register on the r&b listings.

Tina's own postmortem on "River Deep"'s failure was recorded in *Club*. "As far as "River Deep, Mountain High" was concerned, in America, black stations thought it was too pop, and white stations thought it was too black. Consequently, it just didn't seem to get anywhere. It just didn't go at all."

"River Deep, Mountain High," was a resounding flop, but it made Ike and Tina Turner household names. Even now, Tina never goes on stage without performing it. The song was ignored by American radio programmers, yet it is regarded today as a rock 'n' roll classic.

The sequel to the "River Deep" story has become part of rock legend. Spector lost his status as a music business kingpin following the failure of the single. His fall from grace in 1966 was involuntary, but his subsequent total withdrawal from the business was his own idea. Possibly his departure was triggered by the fact that his best effort had been spurned. Perhaps he had lost confidence in himself. Or maybe paranoia had gotten the better of him. In any case, his record company, Philles, went out of business and the man himself, all of 26 years old, retreated behind the electric fence of his mansion in Hollywood, protected by a pack of bodyguards from the hordes of enemies he was sure he had. He has since emerged every few years to make records, but none of his activities since the early 60s have had much impact.

Although "River Deep" went nowhere in America, in July, news of a completely unanticipated development came from England. The record had hit No. 3, right behind The Beatles and The Kinks! While Spector ran a bitter advertisement in the music press ("Benedict Arnold Was Right"), the Turners set out to capitalize on this unexpected new market.

The success of "River Deep" in Britain brought international acclaim to The Ike And Tina Turner Revue. Their continued popularity in England, Australia, and Europe sustained them ever afterwards, even when they found themselves ignored in the States. Years later, after Tina had left Ike, the one place she found complete acceptance was in Britain. It was no surprise that her 1984 comeback started there as well.

The Turners toured in England with The Rolling Stones in 1966 and again in 1968. For the first time, Ike and Tina were playing to predominately white audiences. An ocean away from the racial tensions of America, Tina found herself widely accepted as a unique musical talent. She wasn't what white America saw her as—a tail-wagging black act. She wasn't what black America thought she was—a black act trying to find a white audience. Abroad, Tina was immediately recognized as one of a kind.

Tina theorized about her special appeal to British audiences in a 1984 *Face* interview: "My idea of British people is that they're very correct and hold in a lot, and a lot of what they're holding back is what we (American blacks) put into our music. They tap into what we do because they have so much they suppress. Black people have so much pain from being black and going through what we've suffered; that's soul, and when we sing it's like a lot of those emotions escaping. Maybe that's the connection. I'm sure it would take a psychologist to analyze it properly."

Radio exposure sells records in Britain as well as in the States, and here again Tina found a whole new world. Radio has always been hesitant to play records by unknown artists, but British radio has one attribute the American system lacks: It is color-blind. At the time of "River Deep," there was one official station in the whole of Britain that played rock records (although "pirate" stations beamed rock illegally from boats moored offshore outside the three-mile limit). The single legal station, Radio One, played absolutely all kinds of popular music. It was, and still is, a paradise of variety, with Willie Nelson, Bruce

Springsteen, Billy Idol, and Tina Turner likely to be played consecutively.

The Turners thrived in this accepting climate. There was even another British hit, "A Love Like Yours," which reached No. 16 in December, 1966. The Turners' association with The Rolling Stones led to descriptions of Tina as "the female Mick Jagger"—a label as absurd as the one she now bears: "the black Joan Collins."

The comparison with Mick Jagger was an unavoidable one. "Touring with The Stones, I suppose people sort of figured I was copying from him," Tina said in *Club* magazine. "I've been dancing since I attended a sanctified church in Knoxville way back. I did their dances—as you can tell, they are the basis of some of our routines—but I was too young to understand their religion. But the comparison with Mick doesn't worry me. It's okay, we're good friends."

The Rolling Stones have never been afraid to showcase powerhouse acts on their bill, but following Tina Turner onto a stage certainly requires a lot of self-confidence. However, Jagger and The Stones were so pleased with the warm-up that Tina provided for their audiences during the British tours that they asked the Turners to open for them on their biggest-yet U.S. tour in 1969.

It was the first time The Stones had toured in America in three years, and the demand to see them was intense. As a result, the Turners played before the biggest live audiences of their careers.

"We sort of started in England when we went over to tour with The Rolling Stones," Tina told *Club,* "and when they came to America they asked us to join them again.

At that time we were in the minds of the people, but there were a lot of people who had not seen us before. We were soul singers. You're always given a label. But ever since then we have been drawing more white than black. We still draw a good black audience, but basically I think it's more white than black."

The 1969 tour was perhaps the biggest rock 'n' roll extravaganza since The Beatles' arrival in America. However, the tour is remembered today because of its last and biggest performance, on December 6, 1969, at a northern California speedway called Altamont. The on-camera murder of a young black man by The Stones' bodyguards, the Oakland chapter of the Hell's Angels, earned the concert a place in infamy. The performance was filmed for The Rolling Stones' 1970 rockumentary *Gimme Shelter*, which also features Ike and Tina at their mid-career peak.

Ike and Tina used the wide exposure they had received on the Stones tour to book themselves into mainstream rock venues. Now that they had been discovered by whites, they weren't going to let the whites forget them. It was at this point in her career that Tina made a crucial shift in her repertoire. From here on, the bulk of the songs she recorded came from white sources, either cover versions of hits by white performers or new tunes written for her by white composers. She decided to bring mainstream music back to the mainstream audience—but to bring it back in her own way.

"Proud Mary" was Tina's first vehicle for her assault on the Top 40. John Fogerty's song, originally a hit for Creedence Clearwater Revival in 1969, was a hit all over again for Ike and Tina in 1971. Tina's version, considerably more uninhibited than Creedence's original, reached No. 4 that spring.

"When I first heard Creedence Clearwater singing this song," Tina recalled in an interview on *Friday Night Videos,* "it just took over me. 'Ohhhh, that's the kind of song I want.' I just wanted to sing it.

"It's like that with my life. Any song that I hear that just takes over me, forget it—I don't care if I'm covering it or if someone wrote it for someone else. I want this song for myself, and that's the attitude that I take about that.

"I went to Ike: 'Please let me sing this song.' [I went to him] because Ike was in charge of the repertoire and what was done. He didn't like it ["Proud Mary"]. He couldn't feel what Creedence was doing with it.

"I don't know how long, but later there was a black group that had recorded it on an album, just to fill out a side. Ike could relate more to how that group did it. We took it from there and started strumming it in the car driving back and forth from place to place, and all of a sudden he said, 'O.K., let's put it in the show.'

"We did it two years on stage. And then we signed with Liberty, and the representatives [from the record company] came to see the show. They went, 'Oh! That's it! you've got to record "Proud Mary" and "Come Together" [the Lennon-McCartney 1969 hit].' "Proud Mary" became a hit and "Come Together" made a lot of noise too."

"Proud Mary" was the first positive result of the Turners' new long-term contract with Liberty Records, an offshoot of United Artists. After years of drifting through a series of one-record deals, the Turners had finally reached the point where they could sustain a mainstream career. The Revue had become a professional enterprise, as opposed to a hand-to-mouth operation ruled by Ike's every whim.

Among the popular tunes Tina began reinterpreting during the early 70s were The Beatles' "Get Back" and The Stones' "Honky Tonk Woman." As songs like these burned their way into the nation's subconscious, through Tina's covers and hundreds of others, they began to be considered standards. The Ike And Tina Turner Revue, once the rawest and most unacceptable of r&b acts, soon became a fixture in that great melting pot of American showbiz, Las Vegas.

The money was flowing in now. The Turners built a mansion in Inglewood, a southern suburb of Los Angeles on the edge of Watts, and a recording studio nearby. Those who visited the Turners' home and Ike's studio came away with vivid impressions of bad taste and money wasted.

Like everything the Turners did, the decor was Ike's inspiration. The house contained an indoor waterfall, a dining table cut into the shape of a guitar and a television set that looked like a whale. The one-eyed Moby Dick appeared to be made of ivory but wasn't. Lots of knickknacks around the house appeared to be made of solid gold but weren't. The oft-quoted question about the house was, "You mean you can actually spend $70,000 at Woolworth's?"

Tina later told the *London Evening Standard,* "The house in Inglewood was really Ike's idea. It wasn't to my taste at all. I'd have to say it was a novelty home. To be fair with him, I think he was trying to please me because we'd been to Las Vegas and I'd seen a suite there on the 29th floor somewhere I liked and he just felt that he'd do the house that way.

"But my God, although I said I liked the suite I never said I wanted my home done up like that!"

As for the studio (named Bolic and pronounced nearly the same as Tina's maiden name), it left at least one visitor goggle-eyed. A *New Musical Express* writer described Bolic in 1975: "The building is a most peculiar concoction. As you penetrate its polished hallways, you feel the place would be more suited for building secret munitions than recording albums. . . . Closed circuit television cameras peep over every nook and even some of the crannies. . . . There are even cameras in both the men's and ladies' toilets.

"But in the back nestles the inner sanctum. 'Ike's tomb,' the employees call it in hushed tones. . . . One enters the chamber through ovary-shaped doorways, fitted with doors which look like giant bars of guest soap. . . . There are grotesque red-velvet angry-looking sofas with alien projections which seem ready to suddenly spring and devour an unwary visitor."

Inglewood was by now the base for a well-oiled international machine. In the early 70s, the work was as constant as it had been ten years before, though a higher percentage of the Turners' bookings were for one show a night rather than two. The venues were larger, the audiences were whiter, the dressing rooms were nicer, and the amount of money being made was much, much larger. Ike was totally absorbed with keeping the Revue on the road and in the black.

Tina went along with everything, as she always had. In her 1975 pre-breakup interview with *Club,* she spoke of her dependence on Ike, "as a man, as a musician, as a businessman." Dutifully, she added, "I think every entertainer, male or female, needs that sort of influence. To point out things to you when you aren't aware, little things. Ike can point out so many things to me. Sometimes he might tape me or film me. Then I can see for myself. He watches for things that can be added or taken out of the show to improve it. He controls everything, makes sure the band is giving their all.

Did Tina ever feel like quitting? Her reply to *Club* during the days she and Ike were together was: "Every entertainer and movie star has felt like that at some time in their life. Certainly I did. Often. But what made me go on in those days was Ike. There was always Ike. Music is Ike's life and what he wants. I am a part of Ike—that's what made me go on."

Because she was "the hardest working woman in rock," Tina missed out on a lot of mothering. But she did the best she could, as she told *Club,* given her frequent absences. "I am a very stable person. I think actually I could stop singing today, tomorrow, next week, next year, and be very contented. I have my home, my husband, and my sons. The stage is my work and I enjoy it when I am doing it. I really love it."

The post-breakup interviews cast a much harsher light on Ike and Tina's personal and professional relationship. "I wasn't happy," Tina told *Interview* magazine in 1984. "Ike and I should have remained brother and sister. We were never compatible as man and woman. It was one of those situations where it shouldn't have happened. The love faded after the first several years. It was business, and even then that dissolved itself."

At one point, Tina's suffering became so intense that, in despair, she wolfed down the entire contents of a bottle of sleeping pills just before going on stage. Not surprisingly, the dose left her unfit to perform, and, as she revealed in her interview with *Rolling Stone,* Ike was furious. He beat her up so thoroughly that at one point her doctors thought she might die.

Ike and Tina's career seemed to peak during the early 70s. Some observers, however, contended that the Revue was becoming increasingly jaded. In view of Tina's later disclosures about her state of mind during this period, it would be surprising if the performances hadn't been declining in quality. The energy level remained high, by all accounts, but the spectacle seemed less and less original. Even the infusion of more personal material from the *Nutbush City Limits* album in 1973 couldn't save the Revue from charges of coasting.

Rock 'n' roll, like any activity in life, needs novelty in order to stay fresh. Fortunately for Tina, in 1975, she got a chance to try something completely new—acting.

Ken Russell's film version of The Who's "rock opera" *Tommy* was conceived as a showcase for some of the top names in rock. The Who's vocalist Roger Daltrey would play the lead, as he had on the record. But instead of having Daltrey sing all the parts himself, Russell hired the likes of Eric Clapton and Elton John to fill in where necessary. Ann-Margret and Jack Nicholson, fresh from their triumph in *Carnal Knowledge,* were hired for small parts. When the film came out, though, almost everyone agreed that the show had been stolen by Tina Turner. Her three minutes on screen, during which she played a streetwalker and drug-pusher, showed that her performing range went far beyond her sexy temptress stage image.

Tina had worked in the big leagues before this, supporting The Stones and headlining the big rooms in Las Vegas. Never before, however, had she worked on a basis of personal equality with so wide a selection of showbusiness royalty. Never before had she had so little need for Ike.

As if to demonstrate again that she could be her own person, she was invited to sing a duet with Ann-Margret in a TV special that Ann-Margret taped in England right after *Tommy.* Not only could Tina perform without Ike, she learned, but she could also get work without Ike.

It was new work and it was better work than grinding out yet another edition of "Ike and Tina" for the crowds who didn't know what it was really like to be the Tina half— the lesser half—of the duo. Very soon now, Tina knew, it would be time to declare her independence.

CHAPTER SIX

◇◇◇◇◇

THE STRUGGLE FOR SOLO SUCCESS

◇◇◇◇◇◇

"I started doing TV game shows to pay the rent."

After suffering many years under the domination of her husband, Tina finally summoned up the courage to leave Ike. The following years were difficult ones—Tina had to rebuild from scratch—but she succeeded in establishing her solo career and life.

The early 70s was a time of quiet but radical change in America. Slowly but surely, the goals of the turbulent Sixties were being realized. The black faces at the universities no longer belonged to foreign students. Police cars and mayors' offices began to be occupied by Hispanics. The biggest changes, however, involved women's rights.

But the status of women in The Ike And Tina Turner Revue remained stuck in a Fifties time warp. There was one boss, and his name was Ike. Ike's name always came first in the billing. Publicity pictures always showed the two together, as if Tina couldn't open her mouth and sing without Ike behind her.

Ike was as much a victim as he was a victimizer. He was trapped by the Pygmalion syndrome—the conviction that he, the supreme artist, had created a work of art, and that she existed only through his influence.

By the early 70s, Tina was gradually emerging from the spell Ike had put on her. She could see that women from all walks of life were declaring their independence. One breakup hit particularly close to home: that of Sonny and Cher, a duo whose career in music and on TV showed the Turners what their white counterparts could achieve. When Cher left Sonny in 1974, it made a lot of women stop and think.

Tina, however, was already thinking, and thinking hard. Her recent solo achievements—the success in 1973 of her album, *Nutbush City Limits,* and her electric performance two years later in *Tommy*—proved that she could thrive as a solo act. On a more personal level, she was beginning to realize that she didn't have to settle for any more of Ike's inattentiveness, unfaithfulness, and tyrannical ways.

It was in a Las Vegas penthouse suite that Tina sat down and told the full story of her breakup with Ike. It was 1979, a year that by the standards of 1984 and 1985 seems like a low point in her career, but it was actually a time of renewed hope. She had a new album out, *Rough,* as part of her new solo contract with United Artists. Both her choice of songs and the sound of the album showed that she was fully capable of sustaining a solo career.

She was playing the big room at the Vegas Hilton, and was staying in the plushest suite in the hotel. Wraparound picture windows gave a view of the desert for miles around. It was far from the noise of the slot machines and the roulette tables. What career peaks and downturns lay ahead, no one knew; but for the present things were going very well.

In her penthouse, the once and future queen sat on a couch in the enormous reception room of the suite. At 5'4", Tina is a surprisingly petite woman. Far from reflecting her brassy, suggestive stage presence, her manner in person is mild, even demure. She kept fiddling with a couch pillow in her lap, holding it in front of herself with her arms crossed tightly around it. What she had to say was painful; maybe holding the pillow helped soften her thoughts. Dressed informally and speaking in a low rasp, she told the story of Ike and Tina—the real story she had had to suppress all the time it was happening.

"When I was 30," she began, "that's when I realized that I was fed up, thoroughly. But it took five years for me to take the first step. We had to talk and talk. I kept saying things, and he didn't listen. Then he did listen, and he didn't like what he heard, and he tried to make me stop saying it.

"He pushed me into making the break physical—into walking out on him. I had only left Ike once before. That was for one week, and then three or four years later I left him for good.

"I kept on trying to say, 'Let's work it out, let's work it out together.' He just wouldn't sit down and talk about it. You see, he wanted to control everything. Ike was from the school of the dominant male. To do and to live exactly as he wanted to do and to live—that was his upbringing and his nature.

"Over the years he got a little better than he had been in the beginning. He began to place some little value on my opinion every now and then. He began to be able to listen to what I had to say sometimes. But no matter what my opinion was, it was never better than his opinion. The man was always right—or thought he was.

"This is my idea of it: He had always gone his own way as a musician before I came along, and that's what he kept on doing after we got together. For instance, we'd record a song five or six or maybe even ten different ways in the studio. If I came up with one real good cut and I said I loved it, my opinion made no difference whatever. I began to realize that there was no way out but the door.

"When it came, it was in Dallas. There was a real nice little mess that went on for five hours or more. I wasn't able to go out on stage. It was the second of July three years ago, at the Hilton in Dallas.

"Ike had been up for five days and five nights, and he was tired and irritated. I'd been tired and irritated for 16 years. I wasn't ready to put up with another of his moods. I was in no mood for that. He was real bad to me that day. I felt that it was going to be the last time."

According to Tina's 1984 *Rolling Stone* interview, the final fight in Dallas started out as a routine squabble. The Turners were flying from Los Angeles to play a date at the Dallas Hilton. Driving to the L.A. airport, Ike offered Tina a piece of chocolate. She took it, but it was gooey, and she said something to the effect of "Ick."

So Ike hit her. For some reason, Tina decided she wasn't going to take it any more. The two remained civil while on the plane and in the airport, but as soon as they climbed into the car together after arriving in Dallas, round two of the fight began. And for the first time, Tina hit Ike back. By the time they reached their hotel room, Tina was bruised and bloody. As soon as Ike fell asleep, Tina walked out the door for good.

Endings are often messy but definite. On the other hand, beginnings are usually sweet and dreamy, and happen before anyone realizes what's going on. That's how it was for Tina and Ike. Once she was under his spell, he transformed her into a star. Tina said she loved Ike, but perhaps what she really loved him for was what he had turned her into. Eventually, she realized the only thing Ike had given her was the chance to slave for him.

"I was very much in love with him in the beginning. I went along with everything he came up with, hoping he would change. Well, he didn't change. So I changed.

"Later on, I understood what had happened, how I wasn't allowed to do the things I liked to do or even read the books I wanted to read—I had to sneak them into the house. He became such a negative man. By my second year with Ike I knew that I'd never be happy with him and that I wouldn't stay with him for life. On one level we always stayed good friends, but I knew I couldn't remain with him forever."

Tina became particularly conscious of the difference between the glamorous image that her fans saw and the day-to-day reality that she endured. She remembers, "When I was about 30, I was sitting on a plane looking at the airline stewardesses, who were always so tall and elegant. I sat there next to Ike and suddenly I said, 'Hey, those stewardesses are nothing more than well-dressed waitresses.'

"Ike scolded me for having that idea. He suppressed anything I thought of for myself. And from then on, I started to analyze things and look at them from my own point of view. I started to read things. Here I was a musician and an artist, and I didn't know anything about music and art! I started learning, and I'm still learning, and I want to know more.

"But Ike was totally opposed to any outside things coming in and challenging what he laid down. His only goal was to be involved with music. To him, music was the only good thing, and the only good music was his music. All the time I was saying how I wanted to be an actress. My becoming an actress wasn't Ike's idea of what should happen at all. My thought was that since we weren't progressing too well on records, we should try other avenues—like the movies. Every time I mentioned that, there was trouble. And that's why we got a little stale—we weren't opening ourselves up to anything else but what we'd been doing the same way, over and over, for years."

When Tina left Ike, with the proverbial 36 cents and a credit card in her pocket, she got just what she wanted—nothing, yet everything. She had no cash and no future, just obligations and a vengeful ex-husband-to-be. She had trouble, but it was exhilarating trouble. It was her first chance to breathe fresh air since her teenage years—even though there was every chance she would get blown away. For once she was unprotected by the cocoon Ike had created for her. Could she show the world that she wasn't just Ike's creation, or would she wind up in a "Whatever happened to . . . ?" book.

Everybody took Ike and Tina's break-up hard. Promoters everywhere were reluctant to do business with her, and the fans didn't know what to think. A lot of people took it for granted that Tina wouldn't be heard from again. Wasn't she just Ike's puppet? Had she ever had an idea of her own? Many people thought that her only hope would be to latch on to some other strong man who could tell her to put her left foot here and put her right foot there. . . .

Unbeknownst to almost everybody, Tina wasn't like the dutiful Galatea of the Pygmalion legend, who did everything her master desired. She had more in common with Eliza Doolittle from George Bernard Shaw's *Pygmalion*. Eliza learned everything Professor Henry Higgins had to teach her, and then she left him and never went back.

"I left everything when I left Ike," Tina recalled in that Las Vegas penthouse interview, as the sun went down and the multi-colored lights of the Strip began flashing in the darkness. By 1979 Tina was very much back on her feet, but it had taken more than three years of hard work to get there.

"When I left Ike, I just took my clothes. I really didn't want to lose everything I'd built in 16 years. I knew there would be big losses and a lot of things I'd built up would be damaged, but I never thought it would be as bad as it was. There were two years of awful times for both of us before it was all settled."

The most immediate problem for Tina was rebuilding some kind of home life, and the second was getting work. At home she'd been a little bit of a stranger, and at the office she was just the pretty woman who came in and signed on whatever line Ike pointed to. She had to get to know her own children again. She had to find some friends in the business quickly, because all the industry people that the Turners had dealt with knew Ike, not her.

Tina's first act when she got back to Los Angeles was to move out of the glitzy Inglewood monstrosity that looked more like a set design for a TV game show than it did a home. "I found us a little house in Laurel Canyon, up on the top of the mountain where the trees can grow without being carved to death. It was almost too quiet.

"I got all rented furniture. I didn't have the time or money to bother with curtains. I remember when we first moved in there, lying in the bedroom under the skylight, looking at the heavens. I went to sleep, and then when I woke up I felt something on my face. It was the full moon shining down on me like there was a flashlight on my face. I was scared."

Her fear was a natural reaction. Tina may have chafed under Ike's iron rule, but in some ways, her old life was very easy. She'd had babysitters to watch the children and cooks and maids to handle the chores. Now she had to relearn how to do for herself what had been done for her all those years.

"I was supposed to be starting from scratch, but my head wasn't even into how to start. I had absolutely nothing and no idea of how to get anything. My sister Eileen helped me as far as filling up the refrigerator was concerned. She got me the food stamps so the family could eat something. One thing, I could wash clothes. I never got hung up on that because those years on the road I'd gotten used to doing my own washing. All in all, seeing the comforts I'd given up, we got by all right."

Tina had the right frame of mind for survival. The stick-to-itiveness that Ike had noticed was still there. She had a lot of energy and knew how to apply it to her problems. "I paid a lot of bills. The problems I had at that time really were the same problems everybody has. The biggest problem isn't the bills or anything like that but the tension that goes with that kind of problem. But I had the strength to deal with it. I'd never turned to any of those things that people turn to when they can't deal with their problems. I never smoked, drank, or took drugs."

Tina needed all the strength she could muster, because all of a sudden she was a full-time mother again. It was a shock to Tina—and it was a shock to the four boys. "It was the first time the children and I had spent a long period of time together at home. And it was the first time they had to face the reality of not being rich. I could do it. I was brought up as a country girl, but the kids had been brought up rich. I'd never lost touch with reality, but they had, a little bit anyway.

"The children weren't babies. Two of them were already out of school. They were big little boys. They still test me, but I'm firm with them—firm but fair. I like to laugh and have fun with them, jump up and down on their beds to wake 'em up. My attitude toward the kids is not to be a nag and to stay calm with them. I know when they're lying, and they know it when I know. But I try to do things with no grudge afterwards.

"After I left Ike, the first thing they noticed was that their allowances were missing. They wanted me to buy them everything you could name, and I couldn't. Their lives had been handed to them on a silver platter. I explained what had happened, and they never held any grudge against me on account of what I'd done. They just missed the easy times. I found they were very selfish. I had to go to the mat with them over one or two things. At one point I even moved out, over to the opposite side of town.

"They went through a period of adjustment, getting used to the idea that there wasn't any money for McDonald's, and they had to eat what was in the refrigerator instead. One of them dropped out of school, and I had to send him to this private school in Oregon to get away from the temptation of drugs.

"When I was putting my show back together, I shared my problems with them. They were crazy a lot of times, but we stuck together. It was always a family group. If we went somewhere together, we were together. In airports we would congregate ourselves in one place, and they knew I was in charge and respected me for that.

"Ike had never been around very much to help me raise them. When things used to get really heavy, he might come around and scream at them. First thing, I sat them down and talked to them about how it was time for them to think about getting jobs for themselves and becoming independent. Now that's an idea that's hard to push down a teenager's throat! After about two years, they made their adjustments. They also learned that they could lean on their father too. Everything's calm now. I know what to say to them now when things get a little out of hand: 'You won't get away with using me just because you're men—and they hear what I'm saying.'"

At the same time as Tina was squaring away her new domestic setup, she was dealing with the messy aftermath of Ike. As she said, it was two years of hell. Tina's primary aim was to disencumber herself from Ike, but she found that she couldn't very easily do that on a fifty-fifty basis. So she put the best face on her predicament.

"I said to him, 'You take everything I've made in the last 16 years. I'll take my career.' I didn't even try to get any money from Ike. If I'd fought him, I could have got him to give me some alimony. All I wanted was to start over again, and start over again without him. I wanted to make my own living. I could work, and I did, eventually.

"It's shocking to hear people say how rich I must have been. A lot of it is a mirage. A lot of people who look rich, aren't really. Ike and I did pretty well over the years. There was a lot of property. I wasn't into the exact figures on how much we had. We lived well. I got practically everything I wanted on the material level.

"When it came time to discuss a settlement with Ike, my attorney could not believe it; he absolutely could not believe that I didn't want to fight for the money. But he didn't know me. I'm not a vengeful person. I had no regrets financially about leaving Ike. Money wasn't why I stayed with Ike so long, and I certainly didn't leave him to get more money for myself.

"I didn't leave Ike with him being my enemy. It's very difficult for me to communicate this particular point because apparently it isn't the way other women have felt. The plan I had thought about over the years that I was thinking about leaving Ike—that plan was to leave him and live as a totally free woman.

"I felt I could make it on my own, regardless. I didn't want any long, drawn-out fight with him to hold me back. I was just so happy to be free of him and I didn't feel like going through all those lawsuits. I was advised that I should go through them. I told those advisers how I wanted it done.

"If I'd chosen to fight, the fight would still be going on, because Ike is a fighter. He's the kind of man who wants to win every time. So I said, 'Everything goes.' And everything went.

"I spent a year out of work. A year. When I couldn't find anything, I started doing TV game shows to pay the rent."

Rebuilding her career wasn't as easy as cutting her losses with Ike had been. Once she made the decision not to fight Ike, that problem was settled. Getting back to work, on the other hand, was a long haul, full of uncertainty. But it was also an exhilarating creative challenge: "I found out how much I had to learn after I left Ike. It was like going back to school. I had to be more disciplined and controlled than I ever had been before, because Ike wasn't there to guide me and command me. Jesus, sometimes I felt like stopping, like anybody would."

But she kept working, and slowly, her confidence grew. "I was trying to get a show together on my own. I needed to get myself some music, and I didn't know music. That is, I thought I didn't know music, but I found that I could do it anyway. I thought I had so little knowledge, and it turned out I had a lot of knowledge, without being aware of it."

Nobody puts together a rock 'n' roll show all on her own. For every musician and dancer out on the stage there are a couple of people backstage whose skills are essential.

Tina gives them credit too. "I had a lot of help. Do you think that when you're a star people help you just because you're a star, or just because you used to be a star? It ain't necessarily so.

"The help I got was from people who liked Tina Turner the person, not those who liked Tina Turner the star. One big boost I remember was from Bob Mackie. He's the best costume designer for entertainers in Hollywood. He was a big help in showing me how to dress professionally."

Tina started working seriously on her solo show when she saw her divorce wars were almost through. "When the divorce thing started to get finalized, that's when all this was happening. The show took four months to get off the ground.

"Then I had to start dealing with the concert promoters. I had to get involved in that business, even though I didn't want to. I hate business, but I have to do it. The promoters didn't want to talk to me at first.

"I didn't have a record deal, you see, which is a turnoff for them. I was glad I didn't have a record deal. Our contract with United Artists was up, so I was free to go elsewhere. I knew a recording deal would come along eventually. I wasn't worried about that, particularly because I'm one of those artists that can work without a hit. I don't need to have a song playing every hour on the radio to draw people. The people know they're going to see just as good a Tina Turner show when I don't have a hit as when I do. If I had as many hits as an Elton John, for instance, I'd make a lot more money touring. But even without those hits I can make a good living.

"But the lack of a record deal, let alone hits, was a problem at first because I didn't have any ready answer to the promoters' big question, which was, 'What is she without Ike?'

"I had to prove myself to them. I had to just go out and get on a stage and show them I could do it on my own without Ike. I did it in Fort Lauderdale, Florida, two years ago. After that, I began getting calls from the promoters."

What Tina had shown the promoters and the fans and everybody else was that she could still shake right up there with the best of them, and her voice was as rich and powerful as ever. As soon as people saw her on a stage without Ike, they knew she had more than enough talent to stand on her own. Some even wondered if, after the first few years back in the early 60s, if Tina had really needed Ike at all? Would it have been possible for her to have gone on and become a big success without him?

The question of whether Tina might have been better off leaving Ike earlier is answered by the fact that she started from scratch in the mid-70s and built herself up to the top. After the first few years in the early 60s, virtually everything she accomplished with Ike was Tina's own idea.

"My performance hasn't changed and won't ever change." she says. "My performance was always my own creation. Ike was one of the driving forces. He selected some material. Things were okayed by him. But I did it."

Tina's post-Ike show was designed to stress continuity. The high-energy concept of the show was the same. The songs were largely the same. The girls dancing their frenzied counterpoint to Tina were the same type of girls. The lead guitar work was an exact copy of Ike's.

As soon as Tina put herself back in business, it became just the Tina Turner show. "I hate titles. It's enough to say I'm performing. There doesn't have to be any fancy label. We don't have the 'Ikettes' any more, but we have dancers. The show isn't 'The Revue,' it's just a show. Titles can make a show seem like an in thing. I just go out and do it.

"I got my musicians together. They're a good set of men, and they can play all types of music. Lenny McAloosa, for instance, he's able to duplicate Ike's unique style of guitar playing. I can go there with his emotion, just the way I did with Ike. Ike was a terrific musician. He could really get the audience going. He always had a great band, and those guys knew how to work in his style. But the way my show has developed, the band's playing isn't as important as it was before.

"I have the same criteria for choosing the dancers that I always had. I like 'em pretty. Looks are a necessity for stage work. A mediocre-looking girl who can sing well is good, but a pretty girl who can sing okay is better. I use male dancers now too, and it doesn't matter what color they are. To give you an idea, right now I have two white girls—they're both Jewish but don't look it—and a black guy and a Jewish guy. Out of the four of them, they're all good-looking and only three of them sing well. I'm not naming names!"

Despite Tina's emphasis on continuity, her performances changed perceptibly. She was repositioning herself from a rhythm and blues star who had once had a couple of breakthroughs on the rock charts to a rock 'n' roll singer with r&b roots. The distinction was an important one. It's a transition she might not have been able to make if she had kept on carrying Ike on her back. Slowly, her sound became

63

more mainstream. It would never be anything like elevator music, but the earlier raw edge was off.

For instance, she started singing more ballads. This turned out to be a wise move, for it prepared her for the time when her phrasing would take "What's Love Got To Do With It" to the top. "I like ballads, and that's why I started singing 'em," Tina explains in that way she has of making everything sound perfectly sensible.

"And people like to hear me singing 'em. I sing 'em with a blues flavor. Just because I showed I'm able to sing ballads, that doesn't mean I can't still move. You know that isn't true. I set my image all those years ago as a wild woman. I couldn't ever tame myself. I'm not the type of singer to sit on a stool. I've got to move."

Tina reveled in the freedom she now had, without Ike standing there shaking his head every time a new idea came up. "On stage now, if I decide I don't want to do a particular song, I don't do it. I do a different one. It wasn't that way with Ike, let me tell you. Now I can call the shots myself, and it's a better performance.

"I started back up right from scratch, and I'm doing okay. I don't know how well Ike's doing. I hope he's okay.

"Ike still thinks he possesses me. He still thinks he created me. To him, I'm still his little machine. It's too soon for me to be friends with him. I'm open to it, though. He's a strange, strange but very creative man."

What about other men? Despite her naughty stage persona, Tina is shy, even demure, in person. "When I was with Ike, there never was another man. Right now, I'm not to the point where there would be another man. If there was someone, I'd have to be ready

The good times of the early 1960s are reflected in Ike and Tina's smiling faces. Just a few years after Anna Mae Bullock first sang with Ike, their songs were pounding the charts and Tina was a top star on the r&b circuit.

Ike and Tina (top) and the members of The Ike And Tina Turner Revue.

Tina and the Ikettes at their best—in concert. Though live recordings of The Ike And Tina Turner Revue exist, they fail to do justice to one of the hottest acts of all time.

Ike at the controls. Although Tina stole most of the limelight, Ike generally wrote, arranged, and produced the material, as well as playing keyboard and guitar. He was also well known as a talent scout. In addition to Tina, of course, he helped recruit such r&b greats as B.B. King, Howlin' Wolf, and Bobby Bland to Modern Records.

A glamourous portrait of Tina Turner dating from the mid-1960s. In addition to her powerful, raspy voice Tina took full advantage of her sultry stage presence to keep both her and The Ike And Tina Turner Revue in the public eye.

Ike and Tina Turner in 1973. Shortly after, Tina would leave Ike—
personally and professionally—and set out on her solo career.
Though she was probably entitled to half of their assets, all Tina
took when she left was her clothes. In addition, she spent years
working the club circuit to pay off debts related to a cancelled
concert tour. "It was the price of freedom," Tina explains today.

Above, opposite, and following pages: Several views of Tina in concert, at different times and places in the early 1980s. Though Tina complains she doesn't like to be told how good she still looks ("They think I've just risen from the grave," she told *Interview* magazine), she couldn't help but confirm her status as one of the sexiest performers in rock —no matter *what* the age. "Let's face it," she tells reporters, "I'm naughty, I'm raunchy, and I'm rough."

Tina shows off two of her three '84 Grammy Awards. She won in both the female pop and female rock vocal categories.

Tina Turner proudly holds aloft one of her two American Music Awards at a photo session following the show. Tina won for Favorite Black Female Vocalist as well as the Favorite Black Female Video Artist.

In 1984, Tina opened several concerts for Lionel Richie, and joined him on stage for a few numbers, including a version of Rod Stewart's "Hot Legs," and Richie's own ballad, "Three Times A Lady." Tina admitted the pairing wasn't a match made in heaven, preferring her experience opening for and working with Mick Jagger and The Stones.

Tina Turner and Lionel Richie
congratulate each other after
the Grammy Awards show.
Richie won a single
Grammy for The Album
Of The Year,
*Can't Slow
Down.*

Manager Roger Davies gives a few words of advice to Tina prior to shooting a video for "What's Love Got To Do With It." Directed by 24-year-old Bud Schaetzle, this video was aired only on foreign TV. The video was then reshot by director Mark Robinson.

Tina Turner: The
hardest working
lady in show
business.

to give my life to him. That's the way I am. I'm a one-man woman. I don't fool around. I didn't, and I don't. That's a part of myself that's always been there and still is there.

"When Ike and I got together, I was real young. There was the boy I went steady with when I was in high school, and then there was Ike. Now I'm learning the differences between men—how they have different astrological signs, how they can be different races. I'm courting like a teenager! I'm learning.

"But I'm not having any meaningless relationships —there is no such thing as a meaningless relationship. If it's a relationship, it's meaningful. If it isn't meaningful, it isn't a relationship. I used to say 'I'm not free' when that possibility came up. Now I say that there's no one I've decided to give myself to."

As Tina faced the future without Ike, she knew she had problems, but she also knew she had the right attitude: "It's a new world. I truly see a new world out there that I didn't see before—climates, seasons, people, styles, attitudes, children. I've changed, and the world has changed too. It's not just that women are liberated now, it's the mentality of the men, too. The way the world has changed affected me and other women, and made us feel a lot of new things. I couldn't be like my mother. We can't stay in the same place. Change has to come about."

CHAPTER SEVEN

◆

IN THE RECORDING STUDIO

◆

"We never do nothin' nice and easy.
We always do it nice
and rough."
—from "Proud Mary," *1971*

During the course of their career, Ike and Tina jumped from record label to record label. Their career didn't stabilize until late 1969, when they signed with the Minit label in Los Angeles.

Tina Turner will always remain in Art Lassiter's debt. Lassiter, former lead vocalist of The Trojans and The Rockers, was scheduled to record Ike's latest composition, "A Fool In Love," one day in early 1960. The Kings Of Rhythm were all ready to go that day in St. Louis, and so were The Artettes, Lassiter's female backup group, augmented by The Kings' frontman, Jimmy Thomas.

But Lassiter was nowhere to be found, so Ike decided to try his young protégée, Little Ann, on the number. Ann hadn't been heard on wax since the first version of "Boxtop" was issued on Tune Town a couple of years earlier; Stevens Records head Fred Stevens had already turned down a demo version of what would become "Letter From Tina," claiming "it wouldn't sell because Tina screamed too much."

The end result was a rawer, raunchier sound than anything Ike ever produced. Whatever his protégée may have lacked in polish, she more than made up for in sheer unharnessed energy. Juggy Murray of Sue Records in New York soon came calling at Ike's home on Virginia Place in East St. Louis. Once the rights were sewn up and Little Ann had been reborn as Tina, the song rapidly climbed to the No. 27 spot on the pop charts and went all the way to No. 2 on the r&b lists following its late August release.

The follow-up, a minor-key blues ballad called "I Idolize You," only struggled to No. 82 on the pop charts, although it fared somewhat better with black record-buyers. The next release, "I'm Jealous," sank without a trace.

But with its memorable chunky guitar intro and silly dialogue between Ike and Tina, "It's Gonna Work Out

Fine" (released July, 1961) was a natural crossover item, and its No. 14 pop and No. 2 r&b showing cemented the Turners' reputation as solid hitmakers.

There was only one problem: Ike never uttered a syllable on the tune. Session guitarist Mickey Baker brought the tune to Ike (it was recorded in New York, a rare departure from Ike's St. Louis studio environs), and Baker was forced to take over as co-vocalist when Ike repeatedly couldn't make it through the silly lyrics ("A preacher man? Woman, you must be losing yo' mind!!") without breaking up.

Baker, author of a popular jazz guitar instruction book and New York's top r&b session axeman at the time, was an old hand at these things—his 1956 smash "Love Is Strange," by Mickey and Sylvia, was quite similar to "It's Gonna Work Out Fine." In fact, it's even rumored that Sylvia Vanderpool played guitar on the cut, relegating Ike to the role of producer.

None of the many follow-ups on Sue were quite as memorable, but most possessed the same rough shuffle feel and raw vocals from Tina. "Poor Fool" featured fine support from the girl singers now known as The Ikettes, and hit No. 38 on the pop charts toward the end of '61. "Tra La La La La" made it to No. 50 four months later, and three months after that, "You Shoulda Treated Me Right," which benefitted from hip Ray Charles-styled horn arrangements, hit No. 89.

In the meantime, Ike brought his namesake trio into the studio and cut a single with them, which he then sold to Atco. The Ikettes' "I'm Blue (The Gong-Gong Song)" climbed all the way to No. 19 on the pop charts, making it the Turner organization's biggest hit of 1962. Three Atco follow-ups bombed.

The relationship with Sue Records and Juggy Murray proved the Turners' most stable recording setup until the dawn of the next decade. Five albums were released, plus a greatest-hits collection. Notable cuts include a pair of instrumental showcases for Ike's guitar, "The Groove" and "Prancing" on *Dance*, and the frantic, Little Richard-inspired "This Man's Crazy" by Tina on *It's Gonna Work Out Fine*.

From 1964 on, Ike reverted to his old nomadic style of recording, cutting handfuls of numbers anywhere for anybody, as long as the money was right. A brief reunion with the Bihari brothers at Kent/Modern produced enough material for three albums, including the first live Ike And Tina Turner Revue collection.

The live set was cut at George Edick's Club Imperial in St. Louis, and the Harlem Club, located just across the Mississippi River in East St. Louis, and featured the entire road company. After a spoken admonition from Tina to the unenthusiastic gathering—"In spite of your coldness, I'm gonna try to put on a good show for you"—she launches into James Brown's "Please Please Please," with two extended raps about getting hurt by her man.

Six other vocalists take their respective turns in the spotlight before Tina returns, including longtime Ikette Robbie Montgomery on a good version of "I Love The Way You Love," featuring an impressive solo from Ike. Vernon Guy's version of "For Your Precious Love," wasn't cut live, but at Cosimo's Studio in New Orleans (apparently the tape kept running out during Guy's spots on the show).

Tina finally returns to cover Maxine Brown's "All In My Mind" and closes with the set's lone original, "I Can't Believe What You Say." Considering its catchy melody and overall girl-group sound, the single should have climbed higher than No. 95 on the pop charts in October of 1964.

Another set of live material, *Please Please Please*, presumably dates from the same sessions, but this time, it's all Tina. There are remakes of her two biggest hits, "A Fool In Love" and "It's Gonna Work Out Fine" (Ike doesn't seem to have any problems with the vocal this time around), and a raft of mistitled songs: "The Wedding" is actually Etta James' "All I Can Do Is Cry," while "You Don't Love Me No More" is a cover of Barbara George's "I Know." Sound quality is nothing to brag about on either set.

The Kent studio sides are similar to the Sue material, although Tina seems somewhat restrained by comparison. It is, however, well-produced mid-60s r&b; noteworthy is "Something Came Over Me," a sequel to "It's Gonna Work Out Fine," and there's still another version of "A Fool In Love."

The only reasonably successful single from the Kent/Modern hookup was notched up once again by The Ikettes. "Peaches And Cream" was co-written by producer Steve Venet and Tommy Boyce, who later wrote much of The Monkees' material with Bobby Hart. It rose to No. 35 on the pop charts. Another Ikettes' release, "I'm So Thankful," hit No. 74 seven months later.

Ike was busy hustling his product throughout 1965, although little came of his efforts. He placed a couple of singles on Warner Brothers' Loma subsidiary, including an excellent version of Chuck Jackson's "Tell Her I'm Not Home." Three more 45s emerged on Warner Brothers, and Sue issued another handful, but none of them were hits, either.

71

The enigmatic Phil Spector burst full force into the Turners' existence in 1966. The already legendary producer concocted "River Deep, Mountain High" specifically for Tina, planning it to be his ultimate masterpiece. Spector surrounded her with all his standard accoutrements—banks of soaring violins, thunderous percussion, cavernous echo. Tina wailed her lungs out, and by all rights, it should have been her biggest crossover smash. Indeed it was, in England—and with the critics.

"Tina Turner, who made many records in a shrill, gospel-influenced style, gave herself to the classically trivial lyric with complete abandon, singing high, pure, and with compelling excitement," wrote rock historian Charlie Gillett in his 1970 book, *The Sound Of The City*. "The sound was richer than any producer had yet achieved . . . filling an infinite space around the most impassioned vocal a singer had ever achieved."

Another commentator of the period, Nik Cohn, called Tina "Aretha Franklin's only possible rival" in his 1969 book. *Awopbopaloobop Alopbamboom*. "On "River Deep," she came across as a voice of vast potential, a hurricane, but she must have been Svengalied by Spector because she's never been quite so good again. Usually, she's wallowed in exactly that kind of strangled hysteria that Aretha disdains and it becomes boring. Really, she wastes herself."

For all its dynamic power, "River Deep, Mountain High" only crawled up to No. 88 on the pop charts. Devastated, Spector took a self-imposed two-year hiatus from the recording business.

The Philles album, reissued on A&M, is something of a schizophrenic affair, split about equally between the unique Wall of Sound production techniques that Spector had parlayed into fame and fortune with The Crystals, The Ronettes, and The Righteous Brothers, and some typical Ike r&b productions.

Spector's highlights include a beautiful ballad version of Martha And The Vandellas' "A Love Like Yours," a cover of The Drifters' "Save The Last Dance For Me," and a pair of originals, "Hold On Baby" and "I'll Never Need More Than This," Ike's material features a nice novelty, "Make 'Em Wait" (Ike's deep vocal interjections bring to mind The Coasters), and more remakes of the ever popular "A Fool In Love" and "It's Gonna Work Out Fine" (perhaps Spector should have tried his hand at those two). Actor Dennis Hopper is credited with album photography.

Somewhere along the line, the Turners cut another batch of live material for Warner Brothers, most of it done at the Skyline Ballroom in Fort Worth, Texas, and at Lovann's in nearby Dallas, with production credited to ex-Little Richard mentor Bumps Blackwell.

Whatever Blackwell's role, the Revue hadn't changed much from the Kent days, although sound quality was certainly improved. This is hot, pumping soul, with Tina kicking through Etta James' "All I Can Do Is Cry" and "Something's Got A Hold On Me" and Ray Charles' "Tell The Truth" and "A Fool For You." One selection, "Somebody (Somewhere) Needs You," is obviously a studio production, right down to the fade; the Motownish feel is a definite departure from the Turners' r&b roots.

Frenetic recording activity continued unabated through 1966 and 1967, with the Turners sandwiching sessions for Ray Charles' Tangerine label around an album for Cenco that eventually found its way onto Capitol as *Her Man--His Woman*.

Phil Wright, whose classy arrangements had produced hits for Chess artists including Little Milton, Billy Stewart, and Fontella Bass, wrote some hot horn charts for the album, especially "Get It—Get It," a glorious piece of mid-sixties soul. Much of the set features blues material, which Tina handles effortlessly, and an updated "I Can't Believe What You Say."

All the while, Ike was dabbling with various productions for his own tiny record companies—Sonja, Teena, and Prann. Three Ike and Tina singles graced Sonja, but most issues featured various Ikettes and other Revue artists as vocalists. As Jimmy Thomas recalled in his 1981 *Blues Unlimited* feature, "He had a garage full of unsold records on everybody."

More brassy soul surfaced on unknown labels like Pompeii and Innis, including a solid remake of Bobby Womack's "Nothing You Can Do." Never one to give up on a good song, as his countless remakes would indicate, Ike took a Fontella Bass side he had produced in 1963 called "Poor Little Fool," overdubbed a vocal track sung by Tina five years later, and sold it to Vesuvius Records in 1970.

After being off the pop charts for three years, Tina finally returned in April of 1969 with a heartfelt rendition of Otis Redding's "I've Been Loving You Too Long," which managed a No. 68 showing. Blue Thumb Records convinced Ike to employ an outside producer, Bob Krasnow, who seems to have urged Tina to emphasize whatever blues roots she may have had.

The bizarre album cover (Ike and Tina in whiteface, gobbling watermelon) belies the traditional nature of *Outta Season*. The album presents Tina as an earthy blues belter, a role she's right at home with. Her versions of Sonny Boy Williamson's "Crazy 'Bout You Baby" and Jimmy Reed's "Honest I Do" crackle with energy. Ike's often neglected lead guitar is right up front for a change, and he proves his prowess anew, especially on the solid instrumental "Grumblin"."

The encore Blue Thumb collection, *The Hunter*, is equally sharp, but the title track, originally written by Booker T. Jones for Albert King, only made it to No. 93. The lead guitarist on the next single, "Bold Soul Sister," sounds suspiciously like Texas blues master Albert Collins, who long claimed uncredited participation on the album. This time, the 45 hit No. 59 on the pop charts.

Ike and Tina's checkered recording career finally gained some much needed stability in late 1969 when they signed with the Los Angeles-based Minit firm. Their initial single for the label, released just about the same time their Blue Thumb material was hitting the market, coupled an old Sonja track with "I'm Gonna Do All I Can (To Do Right By My Man)," which claimed production by Memphis stalwart Willie Mitchell. It only made No. 98 on the pop charts.

The first Minit album, *In Person*, went nowhere, but a cover of The Beatles' "Come Together" hit No. 57 in May, 1970. Minit was absorbed by parent company Liberty right around the same time, so the *Come Together* album appeared on Liberty. Their first hit for the firm, a cover of Sly Stone's "I Want To Take You Higher," did still better, rising to No. 34 and remaining on the pop charts for 18 weeks, the duo's best showing since "It's Gonna Work Out Fine" almost a decade earlier.

But nothing equalled the wildly successful revival of John Fogerty's "Proud Mary." From the opening innuendo-drenched warning from Tina—"We never do nothin' nice and easy. We always do it nice and rough"—coupled with Ike's harmonized bass vocals segueing into the brassy hard-charging meat of the tune, the Turners' rendition of the Creedence standard became a classic in its own right. It streaked to No. 4 on the pop charts following its January 30, 1971, release.

The resulting album, *Workin' Together*, contained some of the duo's hottest material, from a spirited revival of Jessie Hill's "Ooh Poo Pah Doo" to a solid slice of Southern soul, "(As Long As I Can) Get You When I Want You." The album also featured original cuts such as "Good-bye So Long," with a King Curtis-inspired tenor solo, the bluesy "The Way You Love Me," and the title track credited to Ike's old pseudonym Eki Renrut.

Then it was Liberty's turn to be absorbed, this time by parent company United Artist. U.A. was immediately successful with a single of "Ooh Poo Pah Doo," which peaked at No. 60. But it was some time before the Turners' had another hit.

Ike and Tina released a first-class live set in 1971. *What You See Is What You Get* was recorded live at Carnegie Hall, and ranks as their best live effort. After a couple of spirited covers by The Ikettes, Tina blasts her way through Arthur Conley's "Sweet Soul Music," The Stones' "Honkey Tonk Woman," and an extended "Proud Mary."

Ike gets some welcome solo space on Bobby Bland's "I Smell Trouble," and his slashing, imaginative playing is greeted with enthusiasm. An eight-and-a-half minute reading of "I've Been Loving You Too Long" borders on the obscene, at least for its era, as the pair get down and dirty. A rousing "Respect" confirms Tina's title as "the hardest working lady in show business."

Another 1971 release, 'Nuff Said, was less distinguished. None of the songs really stand out, though they're competent soul, and the title track is a boring funk instrumental that indulgently fades up and down toward the end.

The Kings Of Rhythm changed their name to The Family Vibes in 1972 and released an unimpressive set of funk instrumentals dubbed *Strange Fruit*. The only halfway memorable selection was a boogie piano piece titled "Bootie Lip," ostensibly a tribute to ex-Kings drummer John "Bootie Lip" Wings, killed in an auto accident more than a decade earlier.

Ike put together an inconsistent but listenable blues album of his own in 1972, *Blues Roots*. Some selections, including the mellow Charles Brown-ish "Broken Hearted" and "Rockin' Blues," are first rate, and Ike's reading of the Five Royales standard "Think" is interesting.

But "If You Love Me Like You Say" is sabotaged by an out-of-place fuzztone guitar, and the bizarre "Right On" consists of little more than four minutes and 45 seconds of Ike chanting the title. Perhaps one interjection during the tune provides a clue: "Things go better with Coke."

Let Me Touch Your Mind, the next Ike and Tina album, was another uneven affair. St. Louis saxophonist-producer Oliver Sain contributed the title soul ballad, and a revival of The Midnighters' "Annie Had A Baby" was harmless fun. But an updated "Up On The Roof" was pointless, and who really wanted to hear Tina emote on "Born Free"?

The World Of Ike And Tina, the pair's first live album since *What You See Is What You Get*, was just as amateurish as its predecessor was polished. The cover of the album promised performances taped in England, France, Germany, and other exotic locales, but most of the record sounds like it was done live in the basement of Ike's Bolic Studios in Los Angeles.

Bad editing, songs fading into one another, and phony crowd noise mar some fairly decent r&b covers from Tina, including Otis Redding's "Just One More Day" and "I Can't Turn You Loose," The Temptations' "I Wish It Would Rain," and two Wilson Pickett covers, "Don't Fight It" and "Land Of 1000 Dances."

Tina finally recaptured the elusive hit formula in the fall of 1973 when her autobiographical *Nutbush City Limits* blasted up to No. 22 on the pop charts. The entire album was a rocked-out affair, including a "River Deep, Mountain High" that owed more to Chuck Berry than Phil Spector and a "Drift Away" that wouldn't make Dobie Gray lose any sleep.

Ike didn't fare as well with his own 1973 effort, *Bad Dreams*, an unpretentious little set that held nothing remotely commercial.

From 1974 until the dissolution of their musical partnership in 1976, it's clear that Ike and Tina had pretty much lost their grip on what would sell. Only two singles graced the pop charts at all—"Sexy Ida (Part 2)," which made a No. 65 showing in November of 1974, and "Baby Get It On," which inched to No. 88 two months later.

Best forgotten altogether is the dreadful *Tina Turns The Country On*, which Ike, to his everlasting credit, seems to have had no role in. Tina moans her way through the likes of "Help Me Make It Through The

Night" and "If You Love Me (Let Me Know)," aided and abetted by studio worthies Tom Scott, James Burton, and Glenn D. Hardin. It's doubtful any of them list this one on their resumés.

Marginally better was *The Gospel According To Ike And Tina*. On paper, it seems a natural—the unbridled energy of Tina tackling standards like "When The Saints Go Marching In" and "Take My Hand Precious Lord." But the proceedings never catch fire, the funk-oriented arrangements don't fit, and Ike's vocal contributions are dismal. "Just A Closer Walk With Thee" must rank among the strangest covers ever committed to wax.

The Turners' long-term contract with United Artists finally expired sometime in 1975 and the pair moved on to the San Fransisco-based Fantasy Records for their final musical collaborations. *The Edge* contained energetic covers of recent rock and soul hits, coupled with more strange blues-based originals featuring Ike.

Tina's versions of Bill Withers' " Lean On Me" and "Use Me" feature sharp horns and heartfelt vocals, while her "Shame Shame Shame" makes the original by Shirley And Company seem tame by comparison. But the album died a quick death after a belated release.

Ike and Tina Turner's peak periods of musical creativity were 1960-63 and 1969-71, but the years in between held more than their share of quality material. The pair's rapid mid-70s artistic decline makes it abundantly clear that Tina was way overdue for a drastic change.

CHAPTER EIGHT

PRIVATE DANCER:

THE COMEBACK

"It wasn't written for me originally, and when I first heard it, I wasn't even sure it suited my style—but I'm sure glad I recorded it!"
—Tina Turner, on "What's Love Got To Do With It"

An exuberant Tina at the 1985 Grammy Award show.

As Tina Turner, provocative in a leather mini-skirt topped off with an enormous teased-out wig, struts on stage to the strains of "Hot Legs," the adoring sell-out house, screaming and whistling its appreciation, instinctively rises to its feet for a heartfelt, pre-show standing ovation. And if anyone deserves it, this legendary performer surely does.

Flashing her famous smile, simultaneously both innocent and wildly lascivious, Tina grabs the mike and yells, "L.A.—it's great to be back!". . . back from the years of despair, the years of endless one-night stands playing to everything from noisy casino audiences to McDonald's conventions, back from the dead. . . . And nothing could be more alive than this ball of high energy on heels as she explodes into a searing, ferocious version of "Proud Mary," the old Creedence hit she's made her own. Fueled by the twin successes of her No. 1 single and album, Tina is white hot—and it shows. Barely pausing to wipe away the sweat before launching into a killer version of "Let's Stay Together," she grabs the mike again, and flexing one of those famous legs against the stand, purrs, "Some people ask me when I'm gonna slow down . . . but you know what I tell 'em? I'm just getting started!"

The audience goes crazy, and small wonder, for, simply put, Tina Turner is a phenomenon. At somewhere around the half-century mark, she looks better, moves better, and sings better that most kids half her age. And as she burns her way through a set that highlights both her r&b roots and her rock 'n' roll instincts, it's hard to believe that just one year ago she was without a record deal in America.

From the vantage point of 1980, it was difficult to imagine the success of 1984. Still deeply in debt following her breakup with Ike, the failure of *Rough* made the prospects of ever landing a major recording deal unlikely. The new decade found Tina alone and hard at work on the cabaret and club circuit, an endless treadmill of gigs that, while paying the bills and keeping her name alive, was also burying her alive creatively. Tina needed someone who could help her direct her energies the way Ike had, but someone who would do it with Tina's best interests in mind.

Tina tried to obtain the services of Lee Kramer, the astute force behind superstar Olivia Newton-John. Kramer declined, but his assistant, Roger Davies, jumped at the chance to work with Tina after being bowled over by her show at the Fairmont Hotel in San Francisco. Davies' backing and belief in her talent gradually allowed her to extricate herself from the supper-club image she'd been saddled with, and re-focus her energies on a more hardcore rock 'n' roll sound and image.

What attracted Davies to Tina was her undiminished vigor and the enthusiastic response of her audience. The key to developing a broad-based popular music career for Tina, Davies recognized, would be capturing her appeal on a record that Top 40 radio stations would program. With this goal in mind, Davies guided Tina away from the knockdown cabaret look that she had thought suitable for a Vegas attraction. He steered her back to rock 'n' roll.

Despite her soul/r&b background, rock 'n' roll—particularly British rock 'n' roll as exemplified by the likes of Mick Jagger and Rod Stewart—had always vied for attention in the Tina Turner songbook, and the transition was a natural move for the singer who had opened for The Stones back in the 60s.

The admiration was mutual, for British fans had long been infatuated with the voice (not to mention the rest of the package) that had carried "River Deep, Mountain High" to the top of the British charts in 1965. So while the U.S. reaction to Tina's new rock 'n' roll direction was less that enthusiastic, fans on the other side of the Atlantic had no such doubts. Catching one of her revamped shows at The Ritz in New York, Rod Stewart wasted no time in inviting her to perform live with him on *Saturday Night Live*. Their electric version of the appropriately entitled Stewart hit "Hot Legs" was quickly followed by another invitation to join The Tartan Terror on stage for his concert at The Forum in L.A. The resulting show was televised via satellite to a worldwide audience of over 40 million people.

Tina's career got another boost in 1982 when she was invited by Mick and the boys to join the Stones on their record-breaking North American tour, a highlight of which was her duet with Jagger on the classic "Honky Tonk Woman."

But despite the fans and the re-awakening media interest in her, Tina was still faced with largely overwhelming disinterest from the powers-that-be—the record labels. Davies, her manager, had made the rounds of all the major record companies, only to find to his undisguised disgust that, "Tina was basically considered to be a has-been. Punk had come and gone, new wave was very big, and they looked at her as some kind of relic from the sixties. I saw her in a completely different light, and always believed she could be huge again, but it was a matter of convincing the labels."

John Carter, then staff producer at Capitol Records (and subsequently the producer of Tina's "Private Dancer" and "Steel Claw" tracks) takes up the story, shedding considerable light on the events prior to the album sessions. "I knew that Roger Davies had offered Tina to a lot of labels—without much luck—and at the same time, I'd heard from various people what a bad idea it was to sign her. Essentially, they'd written her off. There's a great line, 'Once a name, always a threat,' and as a lifelong Tina Turner fan, I was intrigued by the situation."

Carter's interest was further piqued by the fact that Tina's name was by now popping up all over the place. "I happened to go into Tower Records on Sunset, and the kid in front of me was complaining because they were sold out of her old albums—again," he recalls. "I got back to the office, called some other stores at random, and was told the same thing. I then caught her on the Rod Stewart special, where she ate everyone else for lunch, and by now there's a kind of underground buzz. So I did some more checking, and found that she's working some 300 nights a year—to standing room only. Now at this point, she's still signed to EMI in Britain, one of the few places in the world that truly appreciates her, and I find that they've just shot a full-length special of one of her shows which is blowing everyone away. On top of all this, I'd done an interview back in '80 when I was asked to name my three favorite acts to work with, and there was no question—Van Morrison, John Fogerty, and Tina Turner. They're the greatest voices ever. and where are they now? It's ironic, of course, that two of the three have subsequently gone to No. 1 with their biggest chart successes ever."

Despite some scepticism and resistance from his colleagues at Capitol, Carter began pressing for an American deal and championing her cause by searching out new material for her and taking Tina into the house studios to cut some demos. "These tracks later became 'the B-sides,' songs like "I Wrote A Letter" which was the B-side to "Let's Stay Together,"" explains Carter. "It was also a matter of getting her back to recording—and there's nothing like spending money for keeping everyone's interest up," he adds pointedly. "By this time, the company had made a tentative offer, but it was still a matter of sorting out a direction for her that everyone could agree on. Roger Davies had it all very much in focus—he didn't want just another rock 'n' roll record, but a much more contemporary sound. Other people couldn't see it, and meanwhile time was marching on."

"The other interesting point about the behind-the-scenes maneuvering is that now, having agreed to agree on a deal, it was definitely not top priority for Capitol," says Carter. "It got shoved to the bottom of the pile, and that's why I kept taking Tina in the studios to keep the project alive. There were also a lot of personnel changes at the company during this period which didn't help, and ultimately, the new regime tried to back out of the deal. In the end, I had to go through the whole process again, re-selling her to the new people, and in a sense, signing her twice."

Fortunately, Carter's efforts on the American end were boosted by developments in Britain, where Tina was still considered to be a bona fide superstar. In 1982, Tina has been invited by the British Electric Foundation (a production off-shoot of Heaven 17) to sing lead vocals on their reworking of "Ball Of Confusion," the old Temptations' classic. The dynamic cut, released on BEF's *Music Of Quality And Distinction,* was immediately given heavy airplay in Britain, and the Heaven 17 production team of Martyn Ware and Greg Walsh quickly returned the favor by producing a searing version of Al Green's "Let's Stay Together" for her. The single promptly went Top 5 in the British charts, selling over 250,000 copies, and proving beyond any doubt that the singer was anything but a has-been.

"Let's Stay Together," Tina told *Interview,* was a "great song. We didn't change it that much, actually, though Al was singing about one thing and I was singing about something else. You have to get your own meaning in your head. He was caught at the time between whether he wanted to be a minister or in the business. I'm definitely not a minister's wife."

Co-producer Martyn Ware told *The Face:* "She came to us and asked whether we would write a single for her because she'd liked working with us on *Music Of Quality And Distinction*.

"We said yes and then realized we wouldn't have time to write anything properly, so we ended up doing a cover of Al Green's song. She was brilliant, astonishing to work with. Totally professional—a different class compared to anything we were involved with at the moment. Every note she sang was as it should be. We usually have to go through stuff endlessly, correcting it note by note, but she just seems to know exactly what is needed and does it. We got it in the first or second take. We did three or four just for luck, but they were all brilliant."

It was exactly the break Tina needed, as Carter points out. "Over here, they were still pussyfooting around, and suddenly the U.S. was full of imports—"Let's Stay" was happening here as well, especially in the dance clubs. That finally worked everyone up to the fact that she was a hot property again, so they released the single here and at last started talking about recording a full-fledged album."

But by now, riding high on the huge European success of "Let's Stay," Tina was in the middle of a sell-out European tour. "The whole thing came together incredibly quickly, 'cause there literally wasn't any time to do tons of preproduction on the project," recalls Carter. "One day, she was touring, the next day they stuck her in the studios and said, 'You've got two weeks to do it in.'" But Tina never missed a beat, and from a producer's point of view, she's just the ideal artist—just the greatest! She'll do her homework, and when she arrives in the studio, she knows exactly what she's doing." Carter, whose credits include hit albums for The Motels, Sammy Hagar, and Bob Welch, adds that, "Tina's the only artist I've worked with that'll put on the headphones and not ask for different levels, or less snare, or more guitar, etc. It's fine, 'cause she knows the song so well it's completely unnecessary. She'll do everything, including all the ad-libs, perfectly the first time. But of course, none of us have ever been able to resist making her perform it all again!"

"Let's Stay Together" turned out to be Tina's ticket back into the recording business. In the U.K. the single went to No. 6. In the U.S., it was a dance club smash. When Tina came to New York and showed off her style at The Ritz for three sold-out nights, the American recording industry awoke from its stupor. Capitol, the U.S. subsidiary of Tina's British recording company, EMI, decided she still had legs. They gave her $150,000 and two weeks to prove it.

The album of the year—and the comeback of the decade—was not only rushed, but it was also assembled from the jigsaw pieces of no fewer than five producers—John Carter, Rupert Hine, Terry Britten, Martyn Ware, and Greg Walsh; six British studios—The Farmyard, Abbey Road, Mayfair Studios, CBS, Wessex, and Good Earth; and the efforts of 18 songwriters—including David Bowie, Dire Straits' Mark Knopfler, Mike Chapman, and Nicky Chinn.

But while Tina literally studio-hopped from location to location through a bewildering mixture of producers, musicians, and technicians, in order to finish the patchwork sessions within the ridiculously tight schedule, the resulting nine tracks are surprisingly coherent.

"It took about two weeks of meeting with every little producer and little un-producer around and finally making the connection with people like Rupert Hine and Dire Straits," Tina told *Interview* magazine. "They were all very busy and they all made time. Nowadays, people don't move schedules, so I was thrilled."

The album opens with the ironically titled "I Might Have Been Queen," a driving funk-rock number that explores Tina's recent interest in reincarnation, and that celebrates her newfound confidence in no uncertain terms—"I'm a soul survivor/I know the secret combination." The tract was produced by Rupert Hine, well-known for his platinum albums for The Fixx, Howard Jones, and Chris DeBurgh, and co-written by Hine and Jamie West-Oram, The Fixx's guitarist.

"That song was written by Rupert Hine," Tina said on *Friday Night Videos*. "When he produces an artist, he writes the song for an artist. I asked him 'How can you write a song for someone if you don't find out about them and their lives, if you don't have time to spend with them—two or three days?'

"So I sat with him at dinner, and then later on with him at his home. We talked about where I come from, what I like, what I dislike, what I did. When he came up with this song, I went into tears. I really wept for a few seconds. It blew me away. This man saw me. This is a part of me that's real."

Hine plays bass and keyboards, as well as programming percussion on both "I Might Have Been Queen" and "Better Be Good To Me," and joins both Tina and Cy Curnin from The Fixx in back-up vocals as Tina belts out what she describes as "the very rock 'n' roll, very up, very Stones-y feel" of "Better Be Good To Me."

Sandwiched between these two tracks are three songs produced by Terry Britten that provide perfect vehicles for Tina's often underrated vocal range and dynamic control. On the song that finally battered the rest of the civilized world into submission, Tina takes the cool denial of "What's Love Got To Do With It," with its intimation that the attraction is purely physical and sensual, and builds in into an intensely passionate, defensive cry from the heart, a cry that is underscored further by the high-tech moodiness of the synthesizer arrangement.

Ironically, the song that was to catapult Tina to the top of the pop charts for the first time in her 25-year-plus career, and which then went on to win three Grammys—for Record Of The Year, Song Of The Year, and Female Pop Vocal Performance—wasn't automatically a favorite, she later admitted. "It wasn't written for me originally, and when I first heard it, I wasn't even sure it suited my style—but I'm sure glad I recorded it!"

As she explained to *Record*, "The song was this sweet little thing. Can you imagine me singing like Diana Ross or Barbra Streisand, trying to sound velvety and smooth? I really fought. Eventually, we roughened it out instrumentally and I added some phrasings, and we changed the song's attitude and got a hit. I have input, not just in song selection but in treatment too. I'll never be a musician but I know what's right."

In "Show Some Respect," Tina returns to more familiar territory as she belts out her demands against a churning, muscular backdrop of power chords and pounding percussion. These tough, no-nonsense vocals then abruptly switch gears again as Tina dives into the highly effective cover of the Ann Peebles' classic, "I Can't Stop The Rain." With its sparse, haunting instrumentation, the song reveals the singer at her most emotionally raw.

Side two opens with the song that made it all possible, her heartfelt reworking of Al Green's "Let's Stay To-gether" that tastefully and sensitively updates the soul classic with its lush and hypnotic synthesized textures, overlaid with Tina's pleading but assertive vocals. This segues into a fast and suitably savage version of David Bowie's "1984," produced, like "Let's Stay Together," by the Heaven 17 team of Martyn Ware and Greg Walsh who also sing and play on the tracks. Tina spits out the cynical lyrics that seem tailor-made for her with an aggressive abandon that overshadows Bowie's own original version on *Diamond Dogs*.

The album is rounded out with "Steel Claw" and the title track, both of which were produced by John Carter with the added bonuses of guitar solos by the legendary Jeff Beck. Beck was recruited for the sessions after being spotted in the front row of one of Tina's London concerts the year before.

"I'd always been a fan of hers, ever since playing with The Yardbirds and Rod Stewart back in the 60s, so it was great to be asked to play on the album," said the shy guitarist. "We went in and did it all pretty quickly, but it turned out great, and Tina was really pleased. I was so thrilled to work with her that I asked her to sign my guitar—something I never ask anyone to do. Anyhow, she said sure, and sat down on the floor and started rummaging through her bag. I thought she was just looking for a pen or something, but she suddenly pulls out this flick knife and starts carving her name— T-I-N-A—across my beautiful guitar! I was totally speechless, but very proud!" he laughed.

Tina's "penmanship" fortunately didn't prevent Beck from laying down a blistering solo on the breakneck rocker "Steel Claw," or a lyrical and evocative solo on the haunting "Private Dancer," the seven-and-a-half minute epic track that justifiably ends the album with its soaring, swooping, world-weary but ultimately triumphant vocals.

Private Dancer, the album that had taken so long to become a public reality, was finally released worldwide in June, 1984. A full quarter century after first entering the *Billboard* charts with "A Fool For Love," Tina now exploded back on the scene with a vengeance—and chart positions that speak for themselves.

The album raced up *Billboard's* Top Pop Albums chart, hitting No. 3 and staying there for 11 weeks in 1984. It also became one of the longest-running Top 5 LPs, with a consecutive run spanning some 22 weeks over the 1984-85 period. The album also went to No. 1 on the Black Album charts in July 1984—and regained the top spot nine months later, after her Grammy Awards triumph.

The album's singles did equally well, with "What's Love Got To Do With It" zooming to the No. 1 slot on *Billboard's* Hot 100 Singles chart in September, 1984; "Better Be Good To Me" going to No. 5 in November, 1984; and "Private Dancer" hitting No. 7 in March, 1985.

On the Black charts, after the pre-album success of "Let's Stay Together" (No. 3 in March, 1984), "What's Love Got To Do With It" went to No. 2 in July, 1984; "Better Be Good To Me" went to No. 6 in November, 1984; and "Private Dancer" hit No. 3 in March, 1985.

Meanwhile, in the U.K., the album went to No. 1 in September, 1984, spurred by the single success of "What's Love Got To Do With It" (No. 3 in August, 1984). This was followed by more success on the charts with "Better Be Good To Me," "Private Dancer," and "I Can't Stand The Rain."

Meanwhile, with her *Private Dancer* album and singles sales breaking records everywhere, Tina suddenly found herself very much in demand for various music awards shows, where predictably she quickly trounced all opposition and scooped up armfuls of trophies. On January 28, 1985, she performed the album's title track at the American Music Awards and proceeded to win Black Female Vocalist and Black Female Video Artist categories.

But this well-deserved triumph was only a taste of what was to come. A month later, on February 26, at the prestigious Grammy Awards, and in front of an in-house audience of some 6,000 of her peers—and a worldwide television audience of over 150 million—Tina capped one of the most dramatic comebacks in the entire history of the music business by walking off with three Grammys—Record Of The Year and Best Female Pop Vocal Performance for "What's Love Got To Do With It," and Best Female Rock Vocal for "Better Be Good To Me."

"This is the biggest single moment of my career—right now!" the thrilled singer said backstage afterwards. "I've been waiting for this opportunity for a long time—and it really feels good to be back!" But as any Tina Turner fan knows, she's never been away.

CHAPTER NINE

TINA ON SCREEN

"I wanted to be the woman warrior in Conan The Destroyer, *the part Grace Jones got. When I heard about it I said, 'Why didn't they cast me in that!'"*

—Videofile, *1984*

Tina Turner as the terrifying Acid Queen in the 1975 film adaptation of The Who's rock opera, *Tommy.* She hoped that her film career would take off after her mesmerizing performance. It didn't.

Tina is best known as a singer, of course, but her performing talents hardly end there. Though her dramatic credits are few and widely scattered throughout her career, she is a first-rate actress—and always has been.

As she has often said, she acts her songs as much as she sings them. She has made a career out of playing a bold, brassy singer who lights up the stage with her dancing and her singing. The "real" Tina, on the other hand, is quiet, retiring, and contemplative. Like many other singers and entertainers, Tina sells the sizzle that the public expects and demands.

While Tina doesn't yet have the film experience of singers like Diana Ross, David Bowie, Mick Jagger, or Bette Midler, she is appearing this summer in her first starring role in the movie *Mad Max Beyond Thunderdome*, the third in a series of Mad Max films starring Mel Gibson. Tina is billed in the film as "the sexy and deadly Auntie Entity," the strange ruler of a community called Bartertown, and Max's arch-enemy.

Though *Mad Max Beyond Thunderdome* is easily the biggest film role in Tina's career, it's hardly the first. Ike and Tina Turner made appearances in several rock 'n' roll movies in the 60s and early 70s—including Phil Spector's *The Big TNT Show* (1966), *It's Your Thing* (1970), *Gimme Shelter* (1971), *Superstars In Film Concert* (1971), *Soul To Soul* (1971), and *Rock City* (1973). In addition, they made a guest appearance (singing "Goodbye So Long") in *Taking Off*, a 1971 comedy directed by Oscar winner Milos Forman and starring Buck Henry, Lynn Carlin, and Audra Lindley.

Tina's emergence as an actress wasn't recognized, however, until the 1975 release of *Tommy*, director Ken Russell's frenetic adaptation of The Who's classic rock opera. It was Tina's first movie without Ike, and the first chance she was ever given to really act. When the film was being made, Tina knew her departure from Ike was imminent. He didn't approve of her acting ambitions—music was the one and only priority for Ike—and he tried to hold Tina back. She made the movie over his objections, and opened the eyes of both audiences and movie industry insiders.

Producer Robert Stigwood (who had previously brought *Jesus Christ Superstar* to the screen) liked to take chances, and *Tommy* was no exception. He and director-screenwriter Ken Russell agreed that there wouldn't be a single line of dialogue in the entire film, just songs. And Stigwood and Russell went after the oddest collection of singers and actors they could get. Roger Daltrey, lead singer for The Who, made his dramatic debut as the star of the film. Elton John was signed to play the pinball champ who loses his crown to Tommy. Eric Clapton, Keith Moon, Arthur Brown, and Pete Townshend all make appearances. For the crucial role of the Acid Queen, Stigwood first thought of David Bowie. Bowie was anxious to act, and he had a suitably androgynous image. But Stigwood thought better of it and called Tina Turner.

It was a lucky move for Stigwood. Tina's part was short, but she made the best of it, and her scene is considered one of the film's brightest moments. Tommy's parents (Ann-Margret and Oliver Reed) are attempting to cure their son, who is deaf, dumb, and blind. After trying religion, they decide to try pharmaceuticals, and they deliver Tommy into the savage clutches of the Acid Queen, a prostitute and a pusher. She drags Tommy into her lair, ties him down, and shoots him up dozens of times. Tommy staggers home, finds that the net effect of the Acid Queen's terrifying ministrations has been to allow him to look in a mirror and see a red image of his own reflection—nothing more.

Her performance was widely praised, even though some critics noticed that the lip-syncing in her scenes was less than perfect. Still, Tina's portrayal of the Acid Queen was an undeniable highlight. She had invested the weird character with her customary explosion of energy. As she recalled later in *Rolling Stone*: "I became so involved with it that when I had to drag Roger Daltrey up some stairs, I literally dragged his ass up those steps! I really became a madwoman. I think I scared him."

Because the film was so widely seen, Tina's image was given yet a new twist. Not only was she sexually provocative in the film—she'd always been sultry—but she was physically threatening, as well. In the film, she was a huge, looming creature in whose clutches no man was safe. But Tina never got the flood of suitable film offers she had expected. She suggested that she could play the kind of parts that Bette Davis and Joan Crawford had played a generation earlier. Those women, said Tina, had "a kind of strength that comes from knowing who you are."

Because Tina knew who she was, she wanted to play strong roles, like Cleopatra ("I think someone should make that movie with black actors," Tina told the *London Daily Express*), but Hollywood executives felt she was more suited to roles like Cleopatra Jones (the tough government agent played by Tamera Dobson in a pair of early 70s "blaxploitation" films). Actually, when compared to many of the roles Tina was offered Cleopatra Jones was a plum part. "All I was offered were hooker parts," Tina told the *London Evening Standard* in 1978, "and I don't want to be typecast."

When Tina left Ike, all thoughts of a film career had to be put off while she went about the business of getting work and paying off her debts. By the time she was back on her feet, whatever heat *Tommy* had generated for her had long since gone cold. But if Hollywood had forgotten about Tina, Tina certainly hadn't forgotten Hollywood. During interviews in the 80s, she would frequently mention that she was ready and willing to make a movie—if only someone out there were interested.

"I think I'd be terrific in one of those space movies," Tina told *Rolling Stone* in 1981. "Or I could play a really good crook—the girl leading the gang in a western." Three years later, she gave a similar story to *People* magazine. "[Movies are] the enormous leap I'm after . . . I don't want to do sexy movies. And I'm not funny, so I couldn't do comedy. I want to be dealing with some kind of war. Physical strength in a woman—that's what I am."

Talking with *Videofile*, a rock video trade publication, Tina added: "I've been watching horror films—*Conan, The Exorcist*—and that's what I want to do next, be totally inhuman, a fantasy figure. I wanted to be the woman warrior in *Conan The Destroyer*, the part Grace Jones got. When I heard about it I said, 'Why didn't they cast me in that!' And after I do a fantasy part, then maybe I can move on to something more profound. Now I just want to be crazy, that's what I know. Insanity is wonderful for me!"

The one director who heard what Tina was saying was George Miller, an intellectual Australian who has perfected the art of transferring the energy of pulp adventure stories onto the screen. Miller's films include *Mad Max, The Road Warrior*, and the final segment of 1984's *Twilight Zone—The Movie*. His latest is *Mad Max Be-*

yond Thunderdome. Co-directed during 1984 by George Ogilvie, *M.M.B.T.* continues the story of Max (played by Mel Gibson), a former highway patrolman who wanders alone through the burned-out remains of a post-apocalyptic Australia. It is a world where gasoline ("juice") is more precious than gold, where the roads and wastelands are controlled by vicious gangs struggling for survival and control. It is a world of anarchy, greed, and villainy—and also of sacrifice, heroism, and valor.

In the film, Max has been bushwacked and left to die in the middle of the scorching desert. He manages to crawl to "civilization," a weird desert town called Bartertown that's run by Tina's character, Auntie Entity. Max barely escapes with his life, only to have to face Auntie at the film's climax when he tries to rescue a group of children who have fallen in Tina's grasp. Unfortunately, Tina does no singing in this film. Academy Award winner Maurice Jarre is handling the film's musical chores.

For fans who want to see Tina sing on screen, the opportunities are many. Videos of four of Tina's singles from *Private Dancer*—"Let's Stay Together," "What's Love Got To Do With It," "Better Be Good To Me," and "Private Dancer"—have saturated the airwaves, appearing on heavy rotation on MTV and on other music video outlets.

Actually, Tina's first video exposure came in the early 80s with *Nice 'N' Rough*, a one-hour special shot live at London's Hammersmith Odeon in 1981 by video pioneer David Mallet. A performance clip of "Ball Of Confusion" was shot in London in 1982, and a clip from *Nice 'N' Rough* (in which Tina sings her classic composition "Nutbush City Limits") was released in Britain the same year. In addition, Tina has made numerous television appearances on both sides of the Atlantic. But clearly, Tina's four *Private Dancer* videos have been a primary force behind her newfound popularity.

"Let's Stay Together" was shot in London in October, 1983, just prior to the release of the single in Britain. This conceptual video opens with Tina, alone and vulnerable under a single spotlight. The camera pans in and the song's hypnotic groove begins to establish itself. As Tina begins to sing, the camera cuts to various close-ups of men sitting at tables that glow from within, which casts eerie shadows on their faces. As the camera tracks around Tina, it is clear that she's in a very stylized, surreal nightclub, and that the men are now using the glowing tabletops as drums.

The sequence continues as Tina is joined by two back up singers (the girls from her *Nice 'N' Rough* special), and the three dance their way through the next verse and chorus together. At this point, the video cuts to a second set, a futuristic location with tracer lights and a striking sky painted on a backdrop, while Tina and the girls dance and sing in the foreground.

The video clip was directed by David Mallet (who had directed *Nice 'N' Rough* and David Bowie's "Let's Dance," among others) and produced by Pam Jones. The strange concept originally came from Keith Williams, the British video writer whose credits include "Ghostbusters," Billy Idol's "Dancing With Myself," and Phil Collins' "Against All Odds." Interestingly, Williams had developed the concept for a different song and artist entirely. "We'd planned to shoot it as a video for Bob Dylan's "Sweetheart Like You," but he changed his mind just before shooting began," explained Williams. "We even had all the extras sitting around and waiting. So in the end, I just adapted it for Tina and this track, and this turned out even better."

The huge, international success of "What's Love Got To Do With It" spawned not one but *two* different video clips directed by different directors with completely different artistic approaches. American audiences, though, have only seen the second clip shot; the first clip was apparently deemed too "arty" and low-key for the dynamic Ms. Turner.

The first clip was directed by 24-year-old Bud Schaetzle, a graduate of the film school of the University of Southern California. Shot in black and white, Schaetzle's clip is moody and dramatic. Tight shots of Tina singing (bare shouldered and looking very sexy) were intercut with a series of silent vignettes featuring men and women having problems interacting, with Tina walking through the action, the wistful lyrics of the song commenting on the mimed action.

The clip opens with a man lounging at a streetlight. Up above, Tina dabs herself with perfume, slides on a silk stocking, and fixes her earrings. A couple says goodbye beside a cab, as Tina descends a spiral staircase and walks past. In the second verse, the action cuts to a bar scene where a girl slaps a man and promptly bursts into tears. Tina circles nearby, as the camera pans across various characters, each of whom is dramatically lit and noticeably humorless. This scene then dissolves into a models' runway, with girls parading up and down while older women in the audience stare at them. The video clip ends as the camera cut back to the bar scene. Tina leaves the stylized set, passes some men warming themselves at a brazier, and climbs back up the spiral staircase. The final shot lingers on a close-up of Tina's eyes.

The resulting clip, with its emphasis on light and shadow, is stylish and elegant. "The music is very low-keyed which suggests an introspective mood," director

Schaetzle told *Optic Music* magazine. "I'm not much of a video effects fan, and prefer to go with cinematic devices which bring out the subtleties of character." Schaetzle said he used 35mm film because "you can be very subtle with whites, blacks, and grays. And for an artist like Tina, we wanted her to look great when we went in for close-ups, so you could see the fine lines of her hair and that generally sparkling look she has."

The complex video was shot over two long days on a single stage at S&A Studios in Los Angeles. According to Schaetzle, Tina endured the grueling pace like the pro she is. "She has a really enviable quality," he said. "She's able to trust people which allows her to be very open and to let herself go with the action. She never expressed anything other than genuine interest in the project and was really supportive. At no point did she gripe or complain; she was just a real trooper. It's another example of how an established artist who's been around the block a few times can have a much healthier perspective than that of a newer artist."

The second attempt to film "What's Love Got To Do With It," the version familiar to American audiences, was shot a month later in New York by Mark Robinson. It's not that the first video was no good, but Tina and her record company were looking for something more upbeat. They got it, certainly, although the clip's tougher, "I-don't-give-a-damn" depiction of Tina sacrificed some of the vulnerability and introspection that marked Schaetzle's version of "What's Love Got To Do With It."

"It just wasn't me," Tina told *Videofile* magazine about the first clip. "Now I'll sit down with the producers and discuss it with them—the ideas have to come from me so it will be totally my delivery of the song."

And so, Mark Robinson (whose credits include Bob Dylan's "Message Of Love" and The Pretenders' "Brass In The Pocket") took Tina out of the black-and-white fantasy of the studio and placed her at the opposite end of the spectrum: the colorful, gritty streets of New York City. The video opens with the familiar Manhattan skyline and a tug fighting its way upstream. The camera then pans to Tina standing on the shoreline beneath the Brooklyn Bridge dressed in a denim jacket and short leather skirt. She looks tough and street-smart as she struts her way down the towpath, teasingly circling a male pedestrian. She lingers, but only for a second, before confidently heading off again. This Tina may have been hurt in love before, but unlike the first clip, she doesn't look likely to suffer again.

During her walking tour of lower Manhattan (filmed on location over a period of two days) she meets up with a street gang, pushes one tough out of her way, and playfully dances with the others before moving on. During the instrumental portion of the song, there's some great coverage of those famous legs as she sashays down the street. Tina then meets two more characters, lovers quarreling and fighting, and she joins their hands together before walking on to play with some more kids dancing in the street. The video ends as Tina's legs suddenly stop on a child's chalk sketch of her scrawled on the side. She then moves out of frame and disappears.

This version, with its more positive interpretation of the song's melancholy lyrics, gave Tina's hit the visual strength it needed. It also reinforced her image as that of a sensitive and tender woman who is also tough and assertive enough not to get stepped on again.

After three conceptual videos in a row, Tina returned to the familiar concert format for her next video, "Better Be Good To Me." Directed by veteran Brian Grant, the clip was filmed in Septermber, 1984, on location at Los Angeles' Beverly Theater, where Tina was giving a series of sold-out concerts. Appropriately, the clip begins with a shot of the Beverly's marquee—"Tina Turner Live In Concert—Sold Out!"—as the driving beat of the song sets up the action.

The action cuts to the stage of the Beverly and shots of the excited crowd. As the music builds, Tina prowls up and down, an image echoed by the leopards with burning eyes that form part of the stage set. As the song explodes into the hard-rockin' chorus, shots of Tina belting out the lyrics with her typical ferocity are intercut with ecstatic audience reaction shots. The clip also incorporates special guest appearances by two members of The Fixx, lead singer Cy Curnin and guitarist Jamie West-Oram, who both contributed to the album track as well. While West-Oram lets rip with some urgent, slashing guitar licks, Curnin creeps rather mysteriously around the edge of the set. Finally, he joins Tina on stage to romp around a bit and sings the final verses with her.

"Better Be Good To Me" was actually edited and released as two separate clips: a short video produced for MTV and other television outlets; and a longer, dance-club mix that includes more footage of Curnin and Tina dancing together. The latter also expands on Curnin's strange entrance, making the video a bit more coherent. In both versions, Tina is as sexy and dynamic as ever, as she sports tight black leather pants and a matching top.

Just as the *Private Dancer* album reworked Tina's sound, trading in some of her Southern soul and gospel influences for a bit of 1980 synthesizer pop, the video for "Private Dancer" shows us a different side to her on stage persona. Instead of the familiar Tina

Turner—hair flying, hips shaking, high-heeled legs beating a tattoo across the stage—the camera reveals a tired, resigned, dime-a-dance girl of the 1940s, whose only escape is in her flights of fantasy.

The clip opens with Tina looking washed out, nothing at all like her usual "sex goddess" image. Dragging some lipstick across her lips, she walks into the dance hall to begin another evening's work. As the other couples dance around her in slow circles, a customer approaches and presses a dime into her hands. As the song reaches its chorus, Tina is off into her dream world, where she's sheathed in a glittering black sequin dress, and where people dance for art and fun—not for money. As she sings about a husband and a family, images of a bridal couple performing a mechanical dance dissolve into the more erotic suggestions of a man wearing a horned bull's head in silhouette while a woman dances in front of him.

Other dance sequences feature a chorus line being showered with paper money, a little boy and girl dancing, and a series of ballet dancers circling the chair where Tina now lies asleep. As the fantasy ends, she snaps back to the reality of the dance hall, and she recoils in horror, staggering out of the room.

The video not only tells a story, it allows Tina to convincingly construct a believable character around the dance-hall girl. The clip was directed by Brian Grant, one of the best known of all video directors. His other clips include Donna Summer's "She Works Hard For The Money," Peter Gabriel's "Shock The Monkey," Olivia Newton-John's "Physical," and of course, "Better Be Good To Me."

"I've always loved Tina's voice, ever since I first heard her sing "River Deep, Mountain High," said Grant. "When I first heard "Private Dancer," it seemed like another perfect song for her. After all, it kind of mirrors her own life and career over the past few years. She kept working after the break up from Ike—harder than ever, in fact. But it seemed that most of the record industry had written her off as a has-been with no real future in the 80s. But Tina's a tough lady, and she never gave up, and never let go of her dreams."

The clip was filmed in two days at the Rialto Theatre in the London suburb of Lewisham. "Tina was just fantastic to work with, very professional and very cooperative," Grant said. "She's the sort of person who'll try anything to make an idea work, and I think that's obvious from the result."

As for Tina's future in films and video, there should be no shortage of opportunities for either musical outings (she filmed a one-hour special for cable television this spring) or colorful theatrical roles. But what about portraying someone closer to herself? For that matter, would she ever portray Tina Turner if some film or TV project was offered to her?

Tina makes light of such a possibility, though the idea hardly unprecedented. After all, didn't Sophia Loren portray Sophia Loren on a television docu-drama? Reporters covering this year's Grammy Awards asked just such a question of Tina. "Would she star in the colorful story of her own life, if the role was offered?" It would be a great role, Tina's smile seemed to say, though she was somewhat more noncommittal when it came time to go on the record. She merely said: "Oh no, I just lived it. I don't want to go through that again." Take notice, Hollywood. Better luck next time.

CHAPTER TEN
THE WOMAN BEHIND THE MUSIC

*"I'm just going to keep doing what
I'm doing, honey. I'm not going
to change a thing."*
—The Grammy Awards Show, *1985*

On the set of the unreleased version of "What's Love Got To Do With
It," Tina exudes confidence and peace of mind. With the success
Private Dancer, anything seems possible for Tina.

As soon as *Private Dancer* became the hit album of the year, Tina's long and checkered career, which had always been a matter of record, suddenly became prime material for headlines. Her dramatic dismissal of Ike and his abusive ways became a reaffirmation of the strength of womankind. Her practice of working tirelessly in the face of indifference and opposition became an inspiration to the downtrodden. Her undiminished sex appeal became an inspiration to middle-aged people everywhere.

But her main appeal was her new sound. Not only had the instrumental side of her music changed, but the voice, too, was new—more controlled, more masterful. The emotions being expressed were all the stronger for being expressed on a smaller scale.

As Tina said in *Newsweek,* "I never wanted to sing and scream and do all of that wailing, but that was how I was produced in the early days by my ex-husband. I realized I like the way people like Eric Clapton and The Rolling Stones had mixed white and black music, taking feeling from black people and adding it to their own. Blues to me is depressing. White music has a liberating feeling about it, and I needed a change."

Along with a new sound, *Private Dancer* offered a set of songs whose lyrics lent a deeply personal dimension to the album. Despite its many producers and the absence of any Tina-penned material, the collaboration had the feel and the impact of a singer-songwriter's concept album.

As Tina told *Record* magazine, "The songs on the album all relate somehow to the way I lived with Ike and my background before that in the Tennessee fields with my grandmother, and what's happened to me since. It's what I lived through, the different sides of my personality, the performing and spiritual sides. But the final product brings it right back to 1984. There isn't one word on the album that doesn't come back to the way I feel now."

Once the album was released, every commentator who had previously criticized Tina for having "gone Vegas" now lavished her with praise. Critics who had once ignored her because she sounded too black now praised her for her authenticity, while those who had snickered at her provocative act now applauded her age-defying sexiness.

The album was "the first time that the singer has seriously probed beneath her familiar caricature of a sexually voracious rock giantess," wrote *The New York Times* critic Stephen Holden. "Strutting about the stage like an exhibitionistic streetwalker, flaunting a campy sexual challenge and singing with a raucous abandon, Miss Turner seemed to have settled into a comfortable niche as the Mae West of rock 'n' roll." But *Private Dancer* changed all that. "The portrait of Turner that emerges on *Private Dancer* is of a passionate, self-knowing woman who has come through the fire, cognizant in the ways of the world, her spirit undefeated."

As indicated by her success at the Grammy and American Music Awards shows, Tina is no longer the type of artist who periodically surfaces with a song on the radio. She is now a staple, a perennial, a star. "It's beginning to feel like . . . I never really knew what [being] a star is really like," she said in her *Friday Night Videos* interview.

"People do go crazy with the life, and having all the people at their feet. You begin to see why people get blown away with the power of it, if they allow themselves to. There is a certain power. All the 'I' comes in. You got to be very careful.

"I won't get caught up. I didn't get caught up before. I won't get caught up now. I've got a foundation. I'm in control of my life now."

"I'll enjoy it. I'll play with the parameters of it. I'll go very far. But I'll stay right down where we are right now. It's safe."

So far, Tina has remained remarkably unspoiled by her success. After picking up her statuettes on Grammy night, she told reporters backstage, "I'm just going to keep doing what I'm doing, honey. I'm not going to change a thing." Of her awards, she said, "You got to earn one of these. You have to have the material, and now that I've got it, I'm starting to get these.

"You know, I'm really especially happy about this. You have to remember, I never really had a hit record. I've never had a No. 1 record. So this is really special for me."

After more that two decades, Tina has finally come to grips with her provocative image. "[Before] I hated my image because I'm not very tall and the image was this huge wild woman. Millie Jackson is what people expected and then little me would come in and they'd say, 'You lost weight, you've had something done.'

"I'm not raunchy in my real life. I'm not a loud, wild woman. That's who I am acting. That's the other person who I enjoy. And when I'm off, I'm crazy and happy and jolly—maybe a little wild, but it's another kind of wild. It's fun wild.

"You know what annoys me?" she said in *Interview* magazine. "When they come up to me and say. 'You look great.' They think I've just risen from the dead, that I'm this mummy that looks wonderful. God! I haven't died yet, leave me alone.

"Why can't people come up to me and say, 'You're great' or 'Right on'? They look at me and say, 'Boy doesn't she look great.' I could wring their necks. What is all this controversy? I have to make allowances for it, because I have been around a long time. But they're not going up to Mick Jagger and saying, 'He looks great'."

Another contemporary singer, Nona Hendryx, has her own theory on the nature of Tina's sex appeal. Tina, Hendryx said, is "sexier than many of these younger women on the scene will ever be. There's nothing contrived or 'look how sexy I am' about her appeal. It's just there."

With the unprecedented success of *Private Dancer* giving her career and image some richly deserved exposure, a lesser artist might have relaxed a little and savored the success of such a sweet comeback.

But not Tina. Typically, while all this was going on, she was back on the road pursuing a punishing regimen of one-night stands. For two months in the spring of 1985, she underwent a 60-date tour of Britain and Europe.

In Birmingham, England, Davie Bowie joined her to reprise their duet on 'Tonight,' the title track from Bowie's recent album, *Tonight*. They also collaborated on a performance of Bowie's 1983 hit, "Let's Dance." Bowie, no stranger to the limelight, said of the experience, "Standing next to her up there was the hottest place in the universe."

Between live dates, she was back in the studio in England laying down tracks for her next album. Tina is working with the same men who helped her put together *Private Dancer*: Rupert Hine, Terry Britten, John Carter, Martyn Ware, Greg Walsh, and Mark Knopfler. By sticking with her British colleagues, Tina is making a conscious decision to move away from her r&b roots and to further explore the syntho-pop of the 80s.

Her decision to go with a modern, electric sound was not unexpected. In late 1981, she had a chance most singers without an American recording deal would have leaped to grab. Record producer Richard Perry had decided to take Tina up and make her a star again by giving her a new rhythm and blues repertoire. Tina refused.

"Everyone wanted me to do r&b," she said in the *Los Angeles Herald Examiner*. "I didn't want to do r&b. I talked with Richard Perry and did a little work with him, but the producers here [in America] were all of one set, all thinking, 'Here comes the old Tina Turner.' We had to gear ourselves differently."

It's not that Tina doesn't want to sing serious ballads. It's just that she wants to sing them her way. As she told *Interview* magazine, "I like to bring down my high energy show and let people know I can sing. But it's certain types of ballads I want to sing—not real tearful, and not just with a piano, but with the synthesizers and the electric sound. I don't like to get depressed. Ballads can depress you and all of a sudden you get an audience sitting there half-dead, and you've got to pull them out of that mood, because they thought about something that happened years ago."

In certain ways, staying successful is harder than trying to succeed. Remaining at the top requires a different set of skills than getting there. And history has proven time and time again that one platinum album doesn't necessarily guarantee a good reception for the follow-up.

In other words, Tina must progress in order to stay where she is. It's a fact of the business that she's fully aware of. She said in *Record,* "Let's face it I'm naughty, I'm raunchy, and I'm rough. That is, the act—not me. And maybe that'll have to change one day. The voice will change eventually, and I will change too.

"I don't think you can really compare me to anyone else. Nobody does what I do, nobody has a voice like mine, or a life like mine—not even Joan Collins. So whatever life has in store for me ten or twenty years from now, you can't just look at me today and try to plot it out like I was someone else."

Tina's long-harbored desire to become an actress, now being fulfilled by her role in *Mad Max Beyond Thunderdome,* is one of the major changes she's making in her career. "It's something I've wanted to do for quite a long time," Tina admitted to the Australian press. "After all, I'm a very visual performer."

Over the 25 years of her career, Tina has had to undergo more than her share of hardship, disappointment, and suffering. Few people are strong enough to have endured such travails without becoming hateful and bitter. Yet somehow, Tina came through it all seemingly unscathed.

Tina's inner beauty—her strength and self-confidence—are in part a result of her belief in Buddhism. Raised a Baptist, Tina regularly attended church as a child, but in young adulthood found little time for religion. While in her 30s, however, she was attracted to the peace of mind promised by Buddhism. She became an adherent to the faith when she left Ike, after struggling for four years to practice the Buddhist rituals under Ike's disapproving glance.

Buddhism teaches a form of self-motivated predestination: The course of each person's life is set before he is born, but each person has to live his life to the fullest if its potential is to be fulfilled. Tina described her feelings about her adopted religion in the *Guardian*. "It [Buddhism] made me see what I wanted to do with my life. As long as you sit back and just do what your parents or your boyfriend or your husband want you to do, rather than what you want to do, you're never going to be happy."

In *Videofile*, she added: "I was Baptist all my life. I had always lived very straight and honestly, and I had to ask, 'What did I do to deserve all these hardships?' I became Buddhist and began learning about cause and effect. The hardships of life are all things I brought on myself—I don't put the blame on anyone else."

"Until I started chanting, I fought my image," she told *Rolling Stone*. "Now I've come to accept the sweat and the wildness that's Tina Turner. I used to think, 'Why can't I be more like Linda Ronstadt or one of those girls who has it easy and makes all the money? Why do I have to work so hard?' It's because this is what I meant to do in this lifetime, and I'm at ease with that and everything else that used to bug me. Chanting helps get rid of all the crap in my life. It's like turning on a water hose to clean off all the mud."

In her home, Tina worships several times a day at a tall teakwood altar. Her prayers are Buddhist chants, in which the phrase "Nam-myo-ho-renge-kyo" is repeated.

"First of all, " she told *Jet* magazine, "you start feeling a peace within. The normal frustrations that you just have to get up and the day are gone. All of a sudden traffic doesn't bother you—you know how you curse people—you don't go through any of that." Tina's beliefs are so important to her that she often speaks of leaving show business to devote the rest of her life to spreading the word of Buddhism to the uninitiated.

As for Tina's romantic life, the good news is that Tina has quietly found herself a companion, a younger man not in show business. As she said to the *Guardian* in her single days, "I know musicians like a book, and it's one I'm tired of reading. It's a different mentality there—different from a businessman or a regular man; there's too much ego."

"I wouldn't marry another musician," she said in the *London Sunday Times,* "I just want a businessman who's not hung up on fashion and all those things; who'll let me do all of that and just stay in the background, very masculine, very strong."

Tina knew what she wanted all along—to raise herself up without stepping over anyone else to do it. As she told *Record,* "I'm not one of those women crying about how I've been abused by men. I won't put men down. I lived it, and I learned. I always had the control, and eventually all I did was to take it."

Following the success of *Private Dancer,* Tina is at last in control of both her life and her career. Until her 1984 comeback, she'd endured more than her share of pain and hardship. Now, with a voice that's never sounded better and a new career in film underway, Tina's on top of the world. That old "Proud Mary" introduction has never been more true: "It just keeps getting better."

A triumphant Tina
backstage following the
Grammy Awards presentation:
The comeback of the decade!

SELECTED DISCOGRAPHY

TINA TURNER
Albums

Rough .... UA UALA919H
Private Dancer .... Capitol ST12330

TINA TURNER
45s

Better Be Good To Me/
    When I Was Young .... Capitol B5387
Let's Stay Together .... Capitol B5322
Private Dancer/
    Nutbush City Limits .... Capitol B5433
What's Love Got To Do With It/
    Rock 'N' Roll Widow .... Capitol B5354

TINA TURNER
12 Inch Singles

Better Be Good To Me/
    When I Was Young .... Capitol B8609
Let's Stay Together .... Capitol B8579
Private Dancer/
    Nutbush City Limits .... Capitol B8620
What's Love Got To Do With It/
    Rock 'N' Roll Widow .... Capitol B8597

IKE AND TINA TURNER ALBUMS
Albums 1960-1969

Best Of Ike And Tina Turner	Blue Thumb	49
Outta Season	Blue Thumb	BTS5
Get It Get It	Cenco	LP104
Ike And Tina Turner	Cenco	5031
Festival Of Live Performances	Kent	KST538
Ike And Tina Turner Revue Live	Kent	KST514
Please Please Please	Kent	KST550
The Soul Of Ike And Tina Turner	Kent	KST519
Live	KLMP	5014
Ike And Tina Turner Show	Loma	5112
Live Ike And Tina Turner	Loma	5904
In Person	Minit	LP24018
River Deep, Mountain High	Philles	PHLP4001
Cussin' Cryin' And Carrying On	Pompeii	6004
So Fine	Pompeii	SD6000
Dance	Sue	LP2003
Don't Play Me Cheap	Sue	LP2005
Dynamite	Sue	LP2004
Greatest Hits	Sue	LP1038
It's Gonna Work Out Fine	Sue	LP2007
The Sound Of Ike And Tina Turner	Sue	LP2001
Ike And Tina Turner And The Raelettes	Tangerine	15611
Greatest Hits	WB	WS1810
Ike And Tina Turner Show Live	WB	WS1579
Ike And Tina's Greatest Hits	Unart	S21021

IKE AND TINA TURNER
Albums 1970-1980

Sixteen Great Performances	ABC	4014
The Hunter	Blue Thumb	31
Her Man—His Woman	Capitol	ST571
The Edge	Fantasy	9597
Come Together	Liberty	LST7637
Workin' Together	Liberty	LST7650
Airwaves	UA	UALA917
Delilah's Power	UA	UALA707
Feel Good	UA	UAS5598
The Gospel According To Ike And Tina	UA	UALA2036
Greatest Hits	UA	UAS5667
Let Me Touch Your Mind	UA	UAS5660
'Nuff Said	UA	UAS5530

Nutbush City Limits .... UA UALA180F
Sweet Rhode Island Red .... UA UALA312G
Tina Turns The Country On .... UA UALA2006
What You Hear Is What You Get .... UA UAS9953
The World Of Ike And Tina .... UA UALA06462

IKE AND TINA TURNER
45s

Bold Soul Sister/I Know .... Blue Thumb 104
The Hunter/Crazy Bout You Baby ..... Blue Thumb 102
I've Been Loving You Too Long/
    Grumblin .... Blue Thumb 101
Get It—Get It/You Weren't Ready ..... Cenco 112
Betcha Can't Kiss Me/Don't Lie To Me .. Innis 6666
Poor Sam/I Better Get Ta' Steppin' .... Innis 6668
You Can't Have Your Cake/The Drag ... Innis 3002
Chicken Shack/He's The One .... Kent 418
I Can't Believe What You Say/
    My Baby Now .... Kent 402
I Wish My Dream Would Come True/
    Flee Flee Fla .... Kent 457
Please Please Please/
    Am I A Fool In Love .... Kent 409
I Want To Take You Higher/
    Contact High .... Liberty 56177
Proud Mary/Funkier
    Than A Mosquita's Tweeter .... Liberty 56216
Takin' Back My Name/Love Is A Game .. Liberty 56194
Workin' Together/
    The Way You Love Me .... Liberty 56207
I'm Through With Love/
    Tell Her I'm Not Home .... Loma 2011
Somebody Needs You/
    Just To Be With You .... Loma 2015
Come Together .... Minit 32087
I'm Gonna Do All I Can/You've
    Got Too Many Ties That Bind ...... Minit 32060
Treating Us Funky/I Wanna Jump ..... Minit 32077
With A Little Help From My
    Friends/I Wish It Would Rain ...... Minit 32068
Gonna Have Fun/I Don't Need .... Modern 1012
Goodbye So Long/
    Hurt Is All You Gave Me .... Modern 1007
I'll Never Need More Than This/
    The Cashbox Blues .... Philles 135

A Love Like Yours/Hold On Baby ...... Philles 136
A Man Is A Man Is A Man/
    Two To Tango .... Philles 134
River Deep, Mountain High/
    I'll Keep You Happy .... Philles 131
It Sho Ain't Me/
    We Need An Understanding .... Pompeii 66675
You Got What You Wanted/
    Too Hot To Hold .... Pompeii 66682
If I Can't Be First/
    I'm Going Back Home .... Sonja 2001
You Can't Miss Nothing That You
    Never Had/God Gave Me You ...... Sonja 2005
We Need An Understanding/
    Too Many Ties That Bind .... Sonja 5000
The Argument/Mind In A Whirl .... Sue 772
Dear John/
    I Made A Promise Up Above .... Sue 146
Don't Play Me Cheap .... Sue 784
A Fool In Love/The Way You Love Me .. Sue 730
I Idolize You/Letter From Tina .... Sue 735
I'm Jealous/You're My Baby .... Sue 740
It's Gonna Work Out Fine/
    Won't You Forgive Me .... Sue 749
The New Breed/Part Two .... Sue 138
Please Don't Hurt Me/
    Worried & Hurtin' Inside .... Sue 774
Poor Fool/You Can't Blame Me .... Sue 753
Prancing/It's Gonna Work Out Fine .... Sue 760
Stagger Lee & Billy/
    Can't Chance A Break Up .... Sue 139
Tina's Dilemma/I Idolize You .... Sue 768
Tra La La La La/Puppy Love .... Sue 757
Two Is A Couple/Tin Top House .... Sue 135
You Shoulda Treated Me Right/
    Sleepless .... Sue 765
Beauty Is Just Skin Deep/
    Anything You Wasn't Born With .... Tangerine 963
Dust My Broom/I'm Hooked .... Tangerine 967
Baby Get It On .... UA 598
Nutbush City Limits .... UA 298
Ooh Poo Pah Doo .... UA 5078
Sexy Ida/(Part Two) .... UA 528
Up In Heah .... UA 5088
A Fool For A Fool/No Tears To Cry ..... Warner Bros. 5433
Finger Poppin'/It's All Over .... Warner Bros. 5481

122

Ooh Poop A Doo/
    Merry Christmas Baby . . . . Warner Bros. 5493

IKE TURNER AND THE NOTABLE KINGS
OF RHYTHM
Albums

Delta Rhythm Kings Volume 3 . . . . Charly CR30103
Ike Turner Rocks The Blues . . . . Crown 5367
Kings Of Rhythm . . . . Flyright 578
A Black Man's Soul . . . . Pompeii SD6003
Ike Turner &
    The Legendary Kings Of Rhythm . . . Red Lightnin RL0047
I'm Tore Up . . . . Red Lightnin RL0016
Bad Dreams . . . . UA UALA087F
Blues Roots . . . . UA UAS5576
Ike Turner Presents
    The Family Vibes—Strange Fruit . . . UA UAS5560

IKE TURNER AND THE NOTABLE KINGS
OF RHYTHM
45s and 78s

I Know You Don't Love Me/
    How Long Will It Last . . . . Artistic 1504
Nobody Seems To Want Me/
    Nothing But Money . . . . Checker 797
Heartbroken and Worried/
    I'm Lonesome Baby . . . . Chess 1459
Independent Woman . . . . Chess 1472
My Real Gone Rocket . . . . Chess 1469
Rocket 88/
    Come Back Where You Belong . . . . . Chess 1458
Boxtop/Walking Down The Aisle . . . . . . Cobra 5033
The Big Question/Rock A-Bucket . . . . . . Federal 12304
Do Right Baby/No Coming Back . . . . . . Federal 12282
Do You Mean It/
    She Made My Blood Run Cold . . . . . Federal 12297
Gonna Wait For My Chance/
    What Can It Be . . . . Federal 12283
I'm Tore Up/
    If I Never Had Known You . . . . Federal 12265
Just One More Time/
    Sad As A Man Can Be . . . . Federal 12287

Let's Call It A Day/		
Take Your Fine Frame Home	Federal	12272
Much Later/The Mistreater	Federal	12291
You've Changed My Love/Trail Blazer	Federal	12307
Cuban Get Away/Go To It	Flair	1059
Cubano Jump/Loosely	Flair	1040
I Know You Don't Love Me/		
I'm On Your Trail	Royal American	105
My Heart Belongs To You/		
Looking For My Baby	RPM	362
The Way You Used To Treat Me/		
Love Is Scarce	RPM	409
You're Driving Me Insane/		
Trouble And Heartaches	RPM	356
Hey—Hey/Ho—Ho	Stevens	107
Jack Rabbit/In Your Eyes Baby	Stevens	104
Boxtop/Calypso Love Cry	Tune Town	501

IKETTES
Albums

Soul Hits	Modern	MST102
Gold And New	UA	190F

IKETTES
45s

Heavenly Love/Zizzy Zee Zum Zum	Atco	6232
I Had A Dream The Other Night/		
I Do Love You	Atco	6243
I'm Blue (The Gong-Gong Song)/		
Find My Baby	Atco	6212
Troubles On My Mind/		
Come On And Truck	Atco	6223
Here's Your Heart	Innis	3000
So Fine/So Blue Over You	Innis	6667
Camel Walk/Nobody Loves Me	Modern	1003
Da Doo Ron Ron/Not That I Recall	Modern	1024
I'm So Thankful/		
Don't Feel Sorry For Me	Modern	1011
Peaches 'N' Cream/		
The Biggest Players	Modern	1005
Sally Go Round The Roses/		
Lonely For You	Modern	1015
What'cha Gonna Do/Down Down	Phi-Dan	5009
Prisoner In Love/Those Words	Teena	1702

Ike and Tina pose for an
early publicity shot.
Ike was an excellent
talent scout, and knew
that Tina would be a
great asset to his band.

FILMOGRAPHY

MAD MAX BEYOND THUNDERDOME 1985. *Directors:* George Miller and George Ogilvie. *Stars:* Mel Gibson, Tina Turner, Bruce Spence.

TOMMY 1975. *Director:* Ken Russell. *Stars:* Roger Daltrey, Ann-Margret, Oliver Reed, Jack Nicholson, Tina Turner, Elton John, Eric Clapton.

ROCK CITY (a.k.a. SOUND OF THE CITY) 1973. *Director:* Peter Clifton. *Featuring:* The Rolling Stones, Eric Burdon And The Animals, Otis Redding, The Ike And Tina Turner Revue, Pink Floyd, Cream, Stevie Winwood.

SOUL TO SOUL 1971. *Director:* Denis Sanders. *Featuring:* Wilson Pickett, The Ike And Tina Turner Revue, Santana, Willie Bobo, Roberta Flack, The Staple Singers.

GIMME SHELTER 1971. *Directors:* David Maysles, Albert Maysles, Charlotte Zwerin. *Featuring:* The Rolling Stones, The Ike And Tina Turner Revue, The Jefferson Airplane.

TAKING OFF 1971. *Director:* Milos Forman. *Stars:* Buck Henry, Lynn Carlin, Audra Lindley. *Featuring:* Ike and Tina Turner, Carly Simon.

SUPERSTARS IN FILM CONCERT 1971. *Director:* Peter Clifton. *Featuring:* The Rolling Stones, The Ike And Tina Turner Revue, Eric Burdon And The Animals, Donovan, Paul Jones, Arthur Brown, Jimi Hendrix, Otis Redding.

IT'S YOUR THING 1970. *Director:* Mike Gariguilo. *Featuring:* The Isley Brothers, Patti Austin, The Edwin Hawkins Singers, Moms Mabley, The Ike And Tina Turner Revue, Brooklyn Bridge.

THE BIG TNT SHOW 1966. *Director:* Larry Peerce. *Featuring:* The Byrds, Joan Baez, The Lovin' Spoonful, The Ike And Tina Turner Revue, Ray Charles, Donovan, Petula Clark, The Ronettes.

HBO SPECIAL 1985. *Director:* David Mallet. 60 mins.

PRIVATE DANCER 1984. *Director:* Brian Grant.

BETTER BE GOOD TO ME 1984. *Director:* Brian Grant.

WHAT'S LOVE GOT TO DO WITH IT (version II) 1984. *Director:* Mark Robinson.

WHAT'S LOVE GOT TO DO WITH IT (version I) 1984. *Director:* Bud Schaetzle.

LET'S STAY TOGETHER 1983. *Director:* David Mallet.

BALL OF CONFUSION 1983.

NICE 'N' ROUGH 1981. *Director:* David Mallet. 60 mins.

MORE ROCK BIOGRAPHIES AVAILABLE FROM NEL